UNIVERSITY OF MARY HARDIN-BAYLOR

D0560450

TOWNSEND MEMORIAL LIBRARY
UNIVERSITY OF MARY HARDIN-BAYLOR
UMHB STATION BOX 8
900 COLLEGE ST
BELTON, TX 76513

DISCARD

The Emperor's New Clothes

TOWNSEND MEMORIAL LIBRARY
UNIVERSITY OF MARY HARDIN-BAYLOR
UMHB STATION BOX 8016
900 COLLEGE ST.
BELTON, TX 76513

The Emperor's New Clothes

William Kirk Kilpatrick

CROSSWAY BOOKS • WESTCHESTER, ILLINOIS
A Division of Good News Publishers

261.515
K48e

To Robert,
Guy, and Geoff

The Emperor's New Clothes. Copyright © 1985 by William Kirk Kilpatrick. Published by Crossway Books, a division of Good News Publishers.

All rights reserved. No part of this publication may be reproduced, stored in a retrieval system or transmitted in any form by any means, electronic, mechanical, photocopy, recording, or otherwise, without the prior permission of the publisher, except as provided by USA copyright law.

Cover design by Sara Cioni, Cioni Artworks

First cloth printing, 1985

Printed in the United States of America

Library of Congress Catalog Card Number 84-72004

ISBN 0-89107-387-6

The publisher would like to express appreciation for permission to reprint the following:

"Mixing Psychology with Christianity," *The Observer of Boston College,* October 19, 1984.
"On Serving Two Masters," *Lay Witness,* November 1984. Originally appeared in *Catholicism in Crisis,* August 1984.
"The Brahmin in the Bahamas: The Psychology of Selfishness," *Fidelity,* December 1983.
"Why the Secular Needs the Sacred," *The Human Life Review,* Winter 1984.
"Storytelling and Virtue," *Policy Review,* Summer 1983.
"Youth's Frontier—An Evaluation," *Character II,* Winter 1984-85.
"They're Going to Do It Anyway," *Fellowship of Catholic Scholars Newsletter,* March 1984. Originally appeared in *National Catholic Register,* March 11, 1984.
"The Pope's Dream," *Fidelity,* July 1983.
Review of *When Bad Things Happen to Good People,* in *America,* March 26, 1983.
"If I Could Only Live at the Pitch That Is Near Madness," from *Collected Poems 1930-1976* by Richard Eberhart. Copyright © Richard Eberhart 1960, 1976. Reprinted by permission of Oxford University Press, Inc.

TOWNSEND MEMORIAL LIBRARY
UNIVERSITY OF MARY HARDIN-BAYLOR
UMHB STATION BOX 8016
900 COLLEGE ST.
BELTON, TX 76513

CONTENTS

1
The Emperor's New Clothes

T HE EMPEROR'S NEW CLOTHES—not very original, I admit. I can assure you I tried my best to come up with a spanking new title. But sometimes the best way of saying something is the tried and true way. And as a short commentary on our capacity for self-delusion it's hard to improve on Hans Christian Andersen's story of the Emperor, the tailors, the little boy, and the suit that wasn't there.

Like any good piece of mythology, the story has almost infinite application. But it seems to me it has a special application to our current veneration of psychology and psychologists.

Why? Well, because the story is essentially about bowing to expert opinion. It has to do with vanity, and conformity, and foolishness in high places as well; but mainly it's about the folly of letting common sense take a back seat to expert knowledge. If you recall, the ploy used by the swindlers was to claim that the beautiful clothes could only be seen by those who were fit for the offices they held or who were very clever. They could not be seen by anyone who was unfit for the office he held or who was very stupid.

Who can blame the Emperor and his court for being duped? Most of us would much rather be thought very bad than very stupid. The Emperor, despite his vanity, is really a bit unsure of his judgment; so he sends his faithful Minister to check on the progress of the weavers. The Minister, despite his position, is likewise unsure of himself. And so on down the line. Each one thinks, "I can't see anything in this, but who am I to say?" Moreover, by the time the contagion reaches the public, the new enlightened view of clothes-making has the added authority of state endorsement.

Now I wouldn't go so far as to say that psychology is completely naked—that is, completely devoid of truth. There is a solid and growing body of useful facts as well as useful theories and useful therapies coming out of the psychological community. We mustn't forget that. But the greater danger, I think, is not that we won't take psychology seriously, but that we take it too seriously. Because along with the respectable work just mentioned, there is also adrift in the psychological community an abundance of speculation, wishful thinking, contradictory ideas, prejudice, doubletalk, and ideology disguised as science.

In short, the psychological garment, while not completely imaginary, nevertheless has large holes in it. If we fail to notice these holes, it's partly because psychology has achieved emperor-like status in our culture, and partly because all the clever people swear that it's cloaked in handsomely woven ideas. If we are tempted to think, "I can't see anything in this," we are quick to remind ourselves, "but who am I to say?" Our confidence has been overmatched by the force of expert psychological opinion.

The situation we are in concerning our mental health is similar to the situation we are in regarding our physical health. Given the years of training, sophisticated technology, and specialized vocabulary available to doctors, not many of us are inclined to question a physician's diagnosis. The same sort of ultimate expertise now attaches to the psychological profession. And in some ways the psychologist's position is even more secure. After all, if the physician makes a mistake—a faulty diagnosis or the wrong treatment—it soon becomes apparent. But mistakes on the part of the therapist are not as evident. If the client gets worse rather than better, it can be blamed on his own resistance or lack of motivation or some such thing. And if a theorist makes a mistake, it can go undetected for decades.

Despite the overlap between the two professions, however, there is still a basic difference between the physician's expertise and the psychologist's. The physician deals with bones and blood, muscles, organs, and nerves; the psychologist with moods and motivations, memory, thoughts and relationships. Or, to put it more directly, the physician's subject matter can be touched and seen, even if sometimes only with the help of surgical instruments or microscopes. It's another matter with the psychologist's subject field. Who has ever seen an ego structure or an inner dynamic? Much of the psychological garment truly is invisible. Which is not to say there is nothing there—Christians, too, believe in many unseen forces—but rather to suggest that psychology, like Christianity, is partly a matter of faith.

Of course, most people don't regard psychology as a form of religion but as a form of science. They are under the impression that all the theories and therapies are based on research and hard facts. In addition, most of us are somewhat awed by psychology's alliance with the medical profession, and by its alliance with government. Most states have both a department of mental health and a department of social services. And the professionals who staff these bureaucracies have very similar training and views. Both bureaucracies have considerable powers of their own, and in conjunction with the courts their power is nearly absolute. When, in addition to all this power, we consider the prestige accorded psychology by the media, which seek out and amplify every psychological pronouncement or opinion, it is little wonder the average citizen falls into line. If the Emperor and his court insist that he is fully clothed, who are we to dissent?

Except that the subject matters at issue are those things closest to our hearts: our sense of right and wrong, our families, our happiness, our dreams, our purpose for living. Somehow we have been made to believe that psychologists know more about these personal things than we do. The long and short of the psychological revolution is that ordinary people are treated as amateurs in the matter of living their own lives. And the amazing thing is that ordinary people have accepted this professional judgment upon them.

Not that this deference is paid grudgingly. In many, if not most cases, it is paid gladly. Growing up in our culture is truly a bewildering thing. And psychology presents itself to us as a helper. The kind of help it offers comes, moreover, with no strings attached (except the therapist's fee). Psychology purports to be neutral about values. It simply wants to help you make better choices. Exactly what those choices will be is up to you. Or so it seems.

This cloak of neutrality makes it difficult to criticize the flaws in psychology or even to see them. Like medics in combat, psychologists are allowed to go about their business unmolested on the assumption that they are out there just to take care of the wounded. "The moment one admits having a special position," observes Joseph Sobran, "that position becomes vulnerable." But by-and-large the psychological community admits to no special position. They would have us think they are like Red Cross workers. I wish I could say it's a familiar pattern. Unfortunately it's an unfamiliar pattern. Indeed, the success of many liberal and "progressive" movements can be attributed in large measure to their ability to pretend they are not movements at all.

Is psychology neutral? Well, yes, in some respects. In some respects it is what it claims to be, a science and a profession. But if you care to look closely, you will find that in many other respects it looks suspiciously like a liberal and "progressive" movement. And that usually means antitraditional and antireligious.

It is suspicious, for example, that the supposedly neutral values espoused by values clarification curriculums in our schools turn out to be a kind of basic training in relativism. In these classes, choice is elevated to the status of a virtue. In fact, there appear to be *no* other virtues. There are really no right choices or wrong choices in values clarification, just choices that make you feel comfortable or uncomfortable.

Now after a youngster goes through year after year of this and finally grows up to face a real-life moral question, say the abortion issue, he will have developed an almost automatic preference for one side over the other—the side, of course, that favors choice and denies absolutes. In fact, on any number of debates that revolve around the issue of quality of life versus sanctity of life (abortion, euthanasia, infanticide, etc.), the values clarification graduate will be predisposed to the quality of life view. A typical values clarification exercise, for example, gives a description of various passengers on an overcrowded lifeboat and then asks students to decide who lives and who dies. The students are encouraged to view each passenger from the stand-point of utility. The real moral of this little open-ended parable is that some lives are of higher quality than others. It's a loaded game. And I've seen enough of these games played by psychologists that whenever one tells me that such and such "is your choice," I always think of the cardsharp who says, "choose any card."

Despite the obvious bias of values clarification, its proponents have managed for years to convince the public and the public schools of its neutrality. The bias is not confined, however, to this or that school of thought within psychology, but extends to the organizational structure itself. Since we are perhaps more familiar with this kind of bias in other professions, let me mention two other cases first. For example, the National Educational Association, the chief representative of primary and secondary teachers, is anything but neutral. It is notoriously active in liberal political causes, and its lobbying efforts are decidedly—to employ that euphemism again—"progressive."

This is a common pattern for professionals in supposedly neutral fields. Two years ago a study of professionals in media concluded that their political views were well to the left of the average American. And unlike most Americans, religious faith was of little importance to these media elite. In the real world, as we know, beliefs translate into action. Which is why television presents such a badly skewed picture of American life and why it can be doubted that television writers and producers are only interested in reflecting existing values.

7

I don't know if any similar studies have been done to measure the beliefs and attitudes of professionals in psychology and social work, but I'm quite sure I could tell you what they would uncover.* Once you get to know people in these professions, a pattern quickly emerges. It is the same pattern that distinguishes media professionals—that is, a strong preference for what is liberal and progressive, and a strong bias against what is traditional or religious. It shouldn't be surprising, then, that the American Psychological Association requires its members to subscribe to a code of ethics that favors abortion rights, gay rights, and women's rights (of the more radical variety). If this is neutrality, then, to paraphrase Shakespeare, neutrality should be made of sterner stuff.

It may be objected here that psychology is not as antitraditional as I'm making it out to be. One could, for example, point to the increase of family-oriented therapy as a sign of respect for traditional values. To reply to this requires us to shift our focus, or more accurately, to look at two things at once. First, while it is true that family therapists are profamily, they have in mind a somewhat different ideal of family than you or I. Second, the success of their therapy depends on the presence of certain family virtues—virtues which can't be supplied by psychology and which are often attacked by it.

As to the first point, the difference comes down to this: most of us, I believe, when we think of the ideal family, think of one that is bound together by love—a love that we really can't explain because in some ways it goes beyond rationality, requiring as it does such a massive sacrifice of self-interest. Many of us

---

*Since writing this, I have come across such a study. Everett Ladd and S. M. Lippsets' study of the political beliefs of American academics disclosed that among their colleagues in the various disciplines, academics in sociology and psychology hold the most radical political views.

go further and think of family duties as nothing less than sacred duties. Many of us actually take as our model the Holy Family. Though deeply felt, most of this is largely unsaid. It is difficult to be glib about basics.

For example, when we try to give a recalcitrant teenager a reason why he should obey, we often come up with something like, "As long as you live in my house and I pay the bills, you're going to go by my rules!" This is what we say, but it doesn't come close to what we mean. What we really mean cannot easily be put in words and would probably require us to review with our teenager the whole history of his life beginning with his existence in the womb, and then moving on to his life in the cradle and his wobbly first steps. To fully say what we mean, we would then have to go on to talk about the deep mystery of the transmission of life and the fact that due to our love, he will someday inherit a priceless kingdom.

That is not quite the way family therapists view the matter. The ideal family, from the therapist's point of view is, not surprisingly, the therapeutic family. Since the techniques of therapy work reasonably well in therapy, why not in families? In other words, if only parents were more like therapists, how happy we could be. I don't know of any therapist who would put it quite that brazenly, but I do know that is the way their minds often work. And not unreasonably.

For example, one of the most widely used treatment procedures in family practice, and in residential schools and hospitals, is the contract system. Therapist and client draw up a contract that works to both their interests, and agree to abide by its rules. This arrangement tends to make conflict less personal with the result that disagreements can be handled in a more businesslike fashion. As I say, this often works. Therapists then encourage parents to draw up contracts with their children (the same advice now comes in most books on child-raising). Again, this often works quite well, especially when family life had been hitherto unstructured.

The problem arises when the technique is elevated to the status of a philosophy of family life. And once that happens, as I think it has, the nature of the family begins to change. People begin to think it is possible to get rid of all the irrationalities and passions of family life and substitute in their place a cool thera-peutic professionalism. Parents learn parenting skills, and chil-dren learn to honor their contracts rather than their fathers and mothers.

While this approach may work for some families in the short run, the long-run effect may be to undermine all families. There is always a tendency to make a virtue out of a necessity. And this is what seems to be happening. If in the absence of traditional family structures you substitute structures based on contracts and self-interest and if, in addition, these new struc-tures seem to work for families in disrepair, it's easy to go on from there to say that the newer family model is just as good as the old one, if not better.

But that is going a bit too far. The process involves turn-ing a technique into a paradigm. And it involves the error of supposing that structures and attitudes appropriate to one set-ting are appropriate for all. It's like saying that because the Marines are good at instilling spirit and loyalty into young men, families ought to be run like boot camps. You can do that, of course, but don't be surprised if your family begins to resemble a platoon rather than a family. Fortunately the Marines do not insist that the rest of society adopt its ideology and methods. They are too modest. I am not sure the same can be said of psychologists and other helping professionals. They tend to think of all relationships and roles as being culturally condition-ed and infinitely malleable. Hence they do not tremble at the idea of restructuring basic social units. Social change is the most basic thing they know, and their first principle is "adapt to social change."

Every so often a complimentary textbook on child devel-opment or adolescent development crosses my desk. Recently I glanced through six of these, paying special attention to the sections on family life. Apart from the curious language—the home as the most important "agency" in the child's life, the family as the primary "microsystem" in human development—the most remarkable aspect of these texts is the condescending attitude toward the traditional nuclear family and the more than equal time allotted to alternative family arrangements of all types. The words "rapidly changing society" and "remarkable diversity" of family structures run through the texts like a leitmotif. There is no suggestion that trends ought to be reversed, only that they ought to be adapted to.

The question is, where does this lead? Where do we end up if we let social change set all the rules? What happens if there are no absolute standards by which to judge good social change from bad social change? I sometimes wonder what would happen if two-parent families became a small minority in our society. I'm afraid only a few institutions, such as the churches, would still maintain that, fashion or necessity aside, the two parent family is the ideal to which we should aspire. Many in the helping professions have already pounced on the fact that some one-parent families are exceptionally well-run. Are we meant to infer thereby that a one-parent family is as good as a two-parent family? (According to one of the texts mentioned above, "there are no hard data to prove that two parents are better than one at socializing children into becoming vital, creative persons.") This would fit in nicely with many current ideologies.

Some feminists, for example, already believe it. Some even have a preference for one-parent families. And there is no objecting to this view if your model of family life is simply a utilitarian one based on skills, contracts, and results. You can only oppose it from the traditional standpoint that the ideal is a trinity of mother, father, and child, and that somehow this is ordained in the natural and supernatural order of things. This may seem like a weak argument, but actually it's not. It's the same reasoning by which we maintain that two arms is the ideal even though there are many one-armed people who get along quite well. The fact that we can find substitutes or other arrangements to compensate for a damaged limb or a damaged family does not mean we haven't lost something in the bargain. For many purposes an artificial arm is as good as a normal one, but not for a handshake or a caress.

And this brings me to the second point I left unattended several paragraphs ago. The point I made then was that the success of therapy often depends on certain qualities being present in families and individuals—qualities which can't be supplied by psychology. Thus, a whole family may be asked to come to therapy sessions once or twice a week for the sake of one member, and may be asked to "work on" family problems, and may be encouraged to draw up a family contract. But why they should be willing to put in all this time and effort to work on these extraordinarily difficult problems is, from a purely scientific view, a mystery. They do it, of course, because somewhere in their hearts they still bear allegiance to those old notions of family love and loyalty and bearing one another's burdens.

Now psychology may help people to uncover or recover those bonds of love, but it does not forge them. It can even be argued that on one level it acts to undermine them. To put it more accurately, what psychology gives with the one hand, it takes away with the other. What it gives on the individual level with its therapy, it often takes away on the cultural level with its theory. The theory, when it does not totter into some hazy hedonism of self-fulfillment and utilitarian motivations, usually points in the direction of a world increasingly based on management and computer models: a world where people draw up contracts, "interface" with each other, provide feedback, and process information. It is a world strikingly devoid of transcendent meaning, and filled with constant reminders that we only have one life to live (why throw it away on kids?), and constant encouragements to weigh the advantages and disadvantages of relationships.

But anyone taught to seek life's meaning in such terms will, as Ellen Wilson points out, "be at a loss to explain or defend a life which by its nature exacts great amounts of self-abnegation." Psychologists may talk about the "rewards of parenting," but everyone knows that those rewards may include years of ingratitude and heartbreak. Why put up with it? Unless you believe, as Christians do, that the bulk of your reward may be reserved for another life.

In short, there is no rationale in psychological theory for doing the things that therapy demands of families. What there is in all the theory that would make a parent give up time and energy to come to a family therapy session for the sake of a cynical teenager is hard to fathom. Faced with a therapist's demands that he give more love and attention to a child, the psychologically schooled parent of the future could justifiably reply, "That does not compute."

One thinks of Estella in *Great Expectations*. Reproached for her cold heart by her mentor, Miss Havisham, she responds: " 'When have you found me false to your teaching? When have you found me unmindful of your lessons? When have you found me giving admission here,' she touched her bosom with her hand, 'to anything that you excluded? Be just to me.' "

Whether the fact is admitted or not, family therapy relies on the presence of mysteries—mysteries of family love and devotion. Psychological theory, on the other hand, says there are no mysteries. Ironically, the success of family therapy really rests on something other than the psychological mentality, and once the psychological mind-set predominates, family therapy will be a doomed enterprise.

What I am trying to get at here has been nicely expressed (in a slightly different context) by the British historian Christopher Dawson. He wrote: "As liberalism did not create moral ideas, so too it cannot preserve them. It lives off the spiritual capital that it inherited from Christian civilization, and as this is exhausted something else must take its place." What Dawson said of liberalism can be said of psychology. It too lives off the accumulated capital of Christian civilization. It assumes that at heart people want to and will try to act toward each other with what is really Christian love whether or not there is any Christianity around to encourage them.

It goes futher by assuming that the natural hierarchical arrangements of the family can be tinkered with without drying up natural family love. The truth is, it has nothing to offer in place of these except the evanescent promise of some new kind of autonomous person and some new kind of scientific family in which to incubate him. In short, it wants to help us off with our old, unfashionable suit of clothes, and on with a new one which looks suspiciously lightweight and transparent.

We would be wise to question the exchange. Outside the ivory dwelling-places of the experts the weather is often cold and raw, people really do die of exposure, and real cloaks serve better than imaginary ones.

Let me try to put all of the foregoing in some kind of better perspective by raising a practical question. People who are acquainted with my views sometimes ask me if I'm against therapy. Or, more to the point, they will ask if I would advise people to quit therapy. There is no general answer to that question, of course. But I sometimes find it useful to draw an analogy to the welfare system. I ask: "Would you advise an unmarried woman with three small children, no job, and no other source of income to quit welfare?" The answer is usually "No." "Does that mean," I then ask, "that you favor the welfare philosophy and are satisfied with the workings of the present system?" Once again the answer is usually "No." Almost everyone today, whether conservative or liberal, agrees there is something wrong, somewhere, with the welfare philosophy. Though there is little agreement what to do about it, most of us recognize that the system now causes and perpetuates many of the problems it was designed to solve.

The criticisms I level against psychology are of a similar nature. While I wouldn't suggest that people abruptly cut off their supply of therapy, I would suggest that there is something about the psychological mentality and approach which perpetuates and even aggravates the conditions it means to cure. Many ideas which had their start in the psychological community (or received a big boost from it) have now worked their way into the heart of society. I think it fair to say that many of them have wreaked havoc. The subjectivism and relativism of psychological thinking, the confusion about free will, the overemphasis on autonomy and self-acceptance, the denial of guilt, the neglect of and even hostility toward traditional and religious values, the lack of any meaning system to replace these, the transmutation of virtues into hang-ups and perversions into preferences, the undermining of all forms of authority except psychiatric and bureaucratic—all have helped to bring our society to a crisis of catastrophic proportion.

No, I wouldn't advise all clients to stop seeing their therapists. The situation we are in is an ambivalent one. Wheat and weeds have grown up together. But I would suggest that we not let our reliance on (and sometimes affection for) therapists prevent us from looking closely at the quasi-ideological movement to which they belong.

Perhaps the following analogy will be useful in sorting out the confusion. Suppose you are a devout Christian living in some European country close to the Soviet bloc. Suppose further that the local doctor is a devout Communist who would like nothing better than to see your country come under a new social order. When he is not doctoring, he is active in politics; he writes articles and gives talks. Yet he is a good doctor. He has delivered your babies, come in the middle of the night to attend a sick child, perhaps even saved the life of a family member. You have much to thank him for; you can't help but be well disposed toward him as a doctor and as a person.

Because of all this and because of his education, there will even be a temptation to accept his views on a wide range of issues. But that does not for one minute mean that you should. You have an obligation to distinguish between his medical prescriptions and his social ones. And you are well-advised to keep it in mind that if the good doctor's political and philosophical ideas go unopposed, it will likely spell the end of yours. It's also a good bet that if this particular family professional has his way, family life will never be the same.

The analogy to the therapist is not complete, of course. In his case, it is much more difficult to separate his therapeutic prescriptions from his social prescriptions or his treatment from his philosophy. But we should try.

The collection of essays and articles that follow are a step in that direction. They are meant to suggest that when psychologists don the cloak of expert in areas where they have no more authority than the average man—that is, when they invade religion, ethics, and politics—they will often be found upon a closer look to be wearing very little, and sometimes nothing at all.

A few prefaces and waivers first. Since the essays were written at different times and for different audiences, there is some repetition. I beg your indulgence. Also, not all the essays are exclusively about psychology; some deal with the more inclusive secular mentality to which psychology belongs. And not all the criticism is directed at psychology. Two of the essays criticize Christians for getting in the habit of mistaking psychological ideas for Christian ones. Finally, one piece, "The Pope's Dream," represents my attempt at reworking Hans Christian Andersen's tale into a modern context. I think I can safely say it is the only piece of fiction in the following pages. Appearances to the contrary, I did not invent either "The Brahmin in the Bahamas" or "The Quiet Revolutionary."

2
Mixing Psychology with Christianity

C. S. Lewis once said that he preferred to take his Christianity in the same way he took his whiskey—straight. Since Christianity is strong stuff, there is always a temptation to water it down. But, as Lewis realized, the result of such dilutions is a weakened faith.

The current recipe for a Christianity that will travel more smoothly down the gullet calls for blending it with psychology. This mix has become extremely popular with Christian educators, since it seems to add a dash of relevance to the ancient faith. They think of it, of course, not in terms of a dilution, but in terms of the improved product that results when one metal is alloyed with another.

In any event, the practice of blending Christianity with psychology constitutes one of the major trends to have surfaced in American churches over the last thirty years. And it cuts across denominational lines. Catholics do it, Episcopalians do it, even (to paraphrase the old song) evangelicals do it. For example, not long ago a Boston-area priest ended his sermon by concluding that the purpose of Christ's coming was to say, "I'm OK and you're OK." Similar messages abound in the new catechisms. Book Four of the Benziger series for Catholic schoolchildren states that Jesus ". . . was trying to show people how they could be themselves." Book Eight seems to attribute most of Saint Paul's success to his high self-esteem. A study guide for evangelical students goes to great lengths to assure the reader that Moses had "a good self-image." In a recent book a leading Protestant evangelical redefines sin as "negative self-image." And religious educators in both Catholic and Protestant circles seem exceedingly anxious to rework Christian ideas on moral growth in order to make them compatible with the schemes proposed by psychologists Lawrence Kohlberg and Sidney Simon. Sometimes they get rather dogmatic about the new psychology. A parent guide published by Benziger proclaims without qualification that "the conclusions of Kohlberg apply in the case of all human growth." This despite the fact that Kohlberg's conclusions are coming under increasing fire from his fellow psychologists, who apparently are unaware of the *ex cathedra* status of his theory.

What's the harm in all this? Hasn't the Church often grown through the absorption of new ideas? Yes, but the situation appears to be different this time. It's not a case, as it was in the past, of a sure and confident Christianity assimilating pagan practices and philosophies to its own purposes. Rather, it's a case of a confused and conciliatory Christianity willing to lop off limbs from the Body of Christ in order to fit it to a procrustean bed of psychology. Although there is room for some accommodation between Christianity and psychology, there are some areas where it is clearly a matter of either/or. Either the psychologist is right or the Christian is right. Both can't be.

In such cases, attempts to reconcile Christianity to psychology will actually have the effect of undermining the Christian point of view. The most obvious example of this undercutting is provided by the psychological emphasis on self-acceptance. Although there are many kinds and types of psychological theories and therapies, this remains a prevalent theme. It is very nearly the First Commandment of the psychological society that we should accept ourselves as we are. We are urged to greater self-awareness on the happy assumption that we will like what we find. We are, as the saying goes, OK. We just have to learn to be ourselves.

In contrast, Christianity starts off by saying that we're not OK the way we are. There is something wrong with us—a twist in our natures. And the twist is not removed by liking yourself, but by starting to live in Christ. There are plenty of reasons why Christians ought to be happy about themselves, but those reasons are linked to the fact that we've been rescued from the fate of just being ourselves, and they have very little connection with psychological rationales for self-love. Christians are not supposed to facilitate the growth of the old self. They're supposed to give it up and put on a new self. Whether you accept the Christian version of the human situation or the psychological version, one point should be clear: if the psychological point of view is the correct one, then the good news of the gospel is reduced to the status of nice news—"nice" because there was never anything wrong with us in the first place. And if there's nothing wrong with us, why this business about the crucifixion and redemption? OK people don't need a savior.

The main practical effect of this psychological infiltration has been a lowering of the consciousness of sin among Christians. In the Catholic Church, for example, there has been an enormous falling off of the practice of confession over the last twenty-five years. Like everyone else in the psychological society, Catholics have learned to accept themselves. Although this may be good for the ego in the short run, it might be unfortunate for the soul over the long run, since Christ came to save sinners, not self-actualizers. Just as a rich man has a difficult time entering Heaven, so does the fellow who knows nothing but psychological adjustment and self-esteem. Both types are insulated from the saving knowledge of how desperate the human condition is and how utterly dependent they are on God. C. S. Lewis said that "Christian religion is in the long run a thing of unspeakable comfort. But it does not begin in comfort; it begins in dismay, and it's no use at all trying to go on to that comfort without first going through that dismay." This kind of necessary dismay, however, is precisely the thing that the psychological society, with its encouragement to self-esteem and self-sufficiency, is designed to preserve us from.

The contradiction between Christian ideas and ideas cur-

21

rently fashionable in psychology has not escaped the notice of the psychologists. Erich Fromm once observed that if the doctrine of original sin were true, much of his own theory would be untenable. And William Coulson, a former associate of Carl Rogers, recently characterized the encounter movement as "fundamentally anti-Catholic and probably knowingly anti-Catholic on Rogers's part." (Rogers is generally considered to be one of the founding fathers of humanistic psychology.) An obvious question to ask, then, is why so many Christians have been unable to see the contradictions. Carl Rogers remains a favorite with Catholic religious educators, as does Sidney Simon and his system of values clarification, although it is demonstrably anti-Christian. Why do so many Christians insist on blending their faith with psychology?

The answer is that psychology bears a surface resemblance to Christianity. It counterfeits important Christian beliefs. For example, Christianity says that we ought to love ourselves; so does psychology. Christianity says we ought not to judge others; so does psychology. Christianity says we ought to become as little children, and psychology likewise. The fact that these propositions have vastly different meanings in the two traditions doesn't always register. If your mind is set on patching up the differences between Church and world or simply on making people feel good, you will tend to see the similarities and look no further. The wholesale importation of psychological ideas into Christianity would not have occurred if psychology did not have a Christian tone and appearance. Nevertheless, it has not proven to be a prudent venture. It's rather as though the American government were to hire the KGB as chief consultant on ways to improve the American system on the grounds that the Soviets too talk the language of freedom and democracy.

Even supposing, however, that psychological ideas did not flatly contradict Christian ones, it would still be a dubious addition to the fold for another reason. Most psychology is relentlessly reductionistic. It is in the business of reducing things to a size where they can be examined with psychological calipers or fit into psychological categories. For example, a psychoanalytically trained psychologist will tend to look at a great painting not as a reflection of man's search for the Good and the Beautiful, but as a sublimation of the sex drive. In a similar way, when a behavioral psychologist looks at a man offering worship to God, the only explanation he can supply is that the man has been *conditioned* to act that way. The reductionist world view does not leave much room for the Christian view that some things are sacred and therefore on an entirely different level of being. The psychological mind is more comfortable with reducing everything to the same level. For example, a recent news story carried an account of a Catholic nun who has accused the Pope of having psychological problems. This, of course, is a way of reducing the situation, a way of dismissing him and the doctrinal claim that prompted her anger in the first place. No more Holy Father, no more Vicar of Christ, no more keys to the kingdom, just a man with psychological problems.

But this is a rather blatant example. The real danger is more subtle and insidious and has to do with the way even devout and well-meaning Christians allow the faith to be reduced to the level of psychological jargon. The constant reference by Christian educators to "communications skills," "risk-taking," "decision-making," "personhood," "getting in touch," "self-disclosure," "awareness," and so on carries the implication that all the deep mysteries of the faith can somehow be encompassed in secular/psychological categories. After sufficient exposure to this kind of thing, one gets the impression that Christianity is merely a branch of the helping professions.

The irony is that these attempts to blend Christianity with psychology may really have the result of making Christianity not more relevant, but more superfluous. When matters of doctrine are reduced to matters of values clarification and when Sunday school or C.C.D. class comes to resemble nothing so much as a course in communication skills, the average person can be forgiven if he concludes that Christianity has nothing to offer that he can't get elsewhere. The decline in church attendance over the last few decades within those denominations that have leaned most heavily toward psychological awareness does not suggest any reason for thinking that salvation for the churches will come from the direction of psychology. And irony of ironies, while Christians have been busy in their efforts to rid themselves of notions such as sin and guilt, many psychologists have been going in the opposite direction, working to reinstate concepts of sin, guilt, and, yes, even evil (see, for example, Campbell, Gaylin, Coles, Frankl, Vitz, Menninger, Peck). It is a common jibe that the Church is always ten or twenty years behind the times, but in this case it appears to be true. Catholics and other Christians seem to be clambering on board the most shallow-drafted and leaky vessels in the psychological fleet at the very moment the psychologists themselves are abandoning them.

It would, of course, be a pity if Christian educators reacted to these new trends in psychology by playing catch-up once again. If instead of parroting the most recent social science speculations they were to take a closer look at their own tradition, they would find there a more profound understanding of human nature than psychology has yet arrived at. There need be no objection to a truly deep and penetrating psychology, and it is just that—though not only that—that Christianity has always provided.

3

The Brahmin in the Bahamas: The Psychology of Selfishness

While on vacation at a resort hotel in the Bahamas, I found myself seated for lunch with a bronzed, golden-haired psychologist from Arizona, a woman friend of his, and a young couple from Massachusetts. The psychologist noticed that I was reading *Profound Simplicity*.

Now *Profound Simplicity* is an extreme, though not untypical, example of the self-help through positive thinking genre. Among the profound simplicities listed by its psychologist author are the following items.

— There are no accidents.
— Events occur because we choose them to occur.
— Every death is a suicide.
— A rape "victim" is choosing to be raped.
— Social minorities are oppressed only if they allow themselves to be put in a position they call oppression.

"That's a great book, isn't it?" offered the psychologist. I couldn't bring myself to agree with him, and so we fell to talking about psychology. He was in the business of past-lives therapy and had written two or three books on the subject. Most of his inspiration for this had come from Hinduism and Buddhism. I asked if he thought there was anything of value in the Western tradition or in Christianity. Christianity, he explained with an amused smile, makes people feel guilty; guilt is a crippling emotion. The others at the table nodded assent, and the psychologist settled comfortably back in his chair. It was an open and shut case.

I inquired further, "Why are you attracted to the idea of reincarnation?"

"Because," he answered, "it solves the problem of suffering." All his life, he explained, he had been perplexed by the sufferings of the unfortunate and handicapped; the little girl, for instance, who is born crippled. How could such a thing be allowed in a God-governed world? The answer, he discovered, is simple. Everyone gets what he wishes for; some people just aren't very good at wishing. The crippled girl's present sufferings stem from her past life. She is now simply getting what she deserves for failing to make the right choices in her former reincarnation. It is, in short, her own fault.

As I tried to comprehend this resolution to the problem of suffering, the man from Massachusetts began to speak. He had mentioned earlier that he was a computer scientist. Surely, I thought, in the name of science and Yankee skepticism he will voice a dissent. But no. He offers that this is pretty much in line with his own thinking. You're totally responsible for your own life. You choose everything that happens to you, and you pretty much get what you deserve. He had learned this at an est seminar. At this point, his wife, a social worker, added that the same ideas were corrobated by the *Seth Journals*.

"Wait a minute," I protested, feeling faintly like Alice in Wonderland. "You (addressing the psychologist) said you gave up on Christianity because it made people feel guilty, but this is the most guilt-provoking scheme I've ever heard. You're telling this crippled girl, in effect, that she has no one to blame for her handicap but herself."

"From one plane you could call it guilt," he replied calmly, "but it's really just a matter of responsibility. We choose what happens to us. Perhaps she should try harder this time around. People have much more choice than they think; they're just afraid to use it."

By this time, I had had one or two drinks. Tropical drinks taste so sweet that I tend to swallow them right down. A haze of sunshine filtered through the palm fingers above and settled on our table. I noticed that the blue twinkle in the psychologist's eye matched the blue water below. He was a pleasant fellow really. The others at the table smiled benevolently at me. They were nice people, I thought. Maybe they had something there. We sat on a shaded patio, surrounded by palms, looking down at flights of terraced deck descending to the sea: the intellectual class at leisure to philosophize widely. Had I been a Brahmin all along without knowing it? We had found our place in the sun. Surely, we deserved it. Let the others attend more carefully to their affairs . . .

Afterwards, in a more sober mood, I checked through Huston Smith's *The Religions of Man* to see if the psychologist had correctly represented the Hindu position. By and large he had. In explaining the Hindu doctrine of *karma* Smith writes, "The present condition of each individual's interior life—how happy he is, how confused or serene, how much he can see—is an exact product of what he has wanted and got in the past; and equally, his present thoughts and decisions are determining his future states. . . . Each individual is wholly responsible for his present condition and will have exactly the future he is now creating." Crippled girls in Calcutta and thriving Sun Belt psychologists have equally chosen their *karma* and must therefore accept responsibility for their station in life.

TRANSPERSONAL PSYCHOLOGY

This was not my first encounter with Eastern-oriented psychology. A few months before, in the fall of 1979, I had attended the Fifth International Conference of Transpersonal Psychology at a large suburban hotel in Massachusetts. Although the Association of Transpersonal Psychology is an approved branch of the American Psychological Association—the fastest growing branch, they claimed—the convention had a distinctly Eastern tone. Scattered along the carpeted corridors of the Radisson-Ferncroft were a profusion of oriental delights: cow bells from India, pamphlets from a Tibetan monastery, polarity charts on the wall, mantra meditation beads for sale, tofu treats to eat, and yoga classes by the pool.

Among the seminar offerings were the following: "Shamanic and Spiritist Modes of Healing"; "The Tibetan Image of Reality"; "Ancient Indian Concepts of Sex and Love"; "Siddha Meditation"; "Living Tao"; "Archetypical Stages of the Great Round"; "Evolution of a Yogi Trip to Awareness"; "Kundalini Awakening and Spiritual Emergency"; "Aikido as a Spiritual Discipline"; and a dozen or so other topics of a similar nature. The high point of the conference was a special appearance by Swami Muktananda.

It was as though I had wandered into a get-together of the Friends of the East rather than a gathering of mostly-American psychologists. The doctrine of reincarnation was taken for granted here as readily as the benefits of orthodontics are taken for granted at a convention of dentists. The theme of the conference was "The Nature of Reality"; the consensus seemed to be that reality was pretty much an illusion.

Huston Smith, who seems to have been partly converted to Buddhism while his missionary parents were converting the Chinese to Christianity, was there, and so was Carl Simonton, the medical researcher who claims cancer can literally be thought away. Several representatives of Esalen were present, as well as a former senior White House speech-writer and a senior policy analyst for the Department of Education. Many of the speakers were Jungian analysts; one had been a student of Wilhelm Reich.

The keynote address summed up the present state of transpersonal psychology: "From the Fringe to the Center." But this was not completely accurate. An interest in transcendent states had never been far from the center of psychological concerns. Jung had already been there, and Maslow as well. Rogers was more than sympathetic, and Fromm could rarely arrive at a conclusion without hastening to add that The Buddha had been there before him. Whenever, in fact, a psychologist tries to

30

theologize, he comes up with some form of Eastern pantheism. And whenever he seeks a whipping-boy he comes up with the Western tradition. So the Transpersonal Convention did not signify the creation of anything new, but simply the emergence into the mainstream of what had for a long time been a significant element in psychology.

A MARRIAGE OF MINDS

What did it mean, this turn to the East? To begin with, there was a natural attraction, a case of mutual admiration. The humanistic or Third Force psychologists (so named because they represent an alternative to Freudianism and behaviorism, the other two forces in psychology) were much taken with oriental religion. It turned out that the Buddhists and the Hindus were saying practically the same thing as they: God is within—within you and me and everyone; moreover, there are proven ways to unfold this God-power within. Here was a deep sympathy of ideas. What followed this discovery was a matrimony with benefits to both parties. The marriage gave psychology the stamp of ancient wisdom. For the oriental religions, in turn, it brought a handsome dowry: their centuries-old beliefs were now buttressed by the strength of scientific research into the mental health benefits of everything from A to Z—in this case from Aikido to Zen. One result of this merger with the proselytizing spirit of psychology was that the stock of Buddhism and Hinduism began to soar. In the seventies a flood of mystic literature hit the bookstores and a flood of gurus hit the road. The latter teamed up with psychologists and crisscrossed the country, going from conference to workshop to symposium like partners in a traveling road show. The swami and the psychologist—it was an almost unbeatable combination.

There are other reasons for the merger. The exotic and the esoteric are more appealing than the close-at-hand. Psychology had already explained the West to its own satisfaction—had

31

nearly explained it away—and the Western religions seemed all too pat. For a man like Carl Simonton, the son of a minister, the occult proceedings of the Transpersonal Conference must have seemed a marked contrast to the staid practice of middle-class Protestantism. There was nothing in bare-bones Christianity to match the luxuriance of Swami Muktananda's presence.

In one respect, this injection of exotica came none too soon. The turn to the East suggests that humanistic psychology was encountering difficulty in meeting the religious needs of its devotees. By the midseventies cartoonists, comedians, and social commentators were parodying the too-familiar vocabulary and rituals of popular self-help psychology. The movement was in danger of losing its transcendent appeal. The linkup with the mysterious East assured, however, that the supply of startling truths and profound wisdom would not dry up.

Another possible attraction of the merger was this: it gave psychologists the chance to assume the character of wise men. In the Eastern tradition, the guru had a legitimate role. Few others were accorded the honor and reverence given to the holy men of Japan, China, and India. A psychologist then could continue in good secular fashion to refuse the role of priest with its dogmatic connotations, while taking up the role of spiritual guide. Many did so. A few, like Richard Alpert (the Harvard psychologist who disappeared and resurfaced as Baba Ram Dass), went so far as to change their identities completely.

GETTING TIRED

But the lure of the exotic is, at best, a superficial one. A deeper, more theological warrant for the union presented itself. It solved a difficult canonical and practical problem that had cropped up in psychological thinking and doing.

Humanistic psychology had championed an evangelical cause: the radical transformation of the person, the sign and seal of which was a high pitch of emotional intensity. Such a level of feeling, however, is difficult enough to maintain even for Pentecostals, who at least have the aid of the Holy Spirit. When the entire burden devolves on the self alone, something may give. Something like this seems to have happened, for example, in the encounter group movement. It was observed that the same people would pop up time after time at different encounters across the country, seeking booster shots of joy. Something wasn't working. As the painstaking research by Irving Yalom and his associates suggested, encounter was not changing people's lives. Instead, it appeared that people were getting tired of being spontaneously and vibrantly human.

Esalen itself, the high temple of the movement, began to suffer from boredom. The community that once vibrated to the beat of Fritz Perls had by 1979 become "a nice village filled with friendly, bored people . . . a little on the dull side." In an attempt to get back the old thrill, Esalen, which had already at times taken on the atmosphere of an ashram, allowed itself to go fully mystical. Enter Jenny O'Connor, a young Englishwoman who within a year became the Institute's guiding light. Miss O'Connor, a psychic, claimed to be in touch with "The Nine"—"a group of eight-million-year-old mass-energy entities from the star Sirius." Appearing mainly to Miss O'Connor, but also to select other members in flashes of white light, "The Nine" succeeded in reorganizing the entire management of the Institute. Their main task, it seems, was to weed out the burned-out cases and to promote the enthusiasts.

JUST LET IT BE

The experience at Esalen illustrates a general problem. Radical transformation of the self is a difficult burden to sustain. Gradually a new idea began to assert itself: why not an evolutionary transformation instead of a revolutionary one? Why not allow the human personality several lifetimes to accomplish pefection? Why not, in short, substitute an Eastern idea for a Western one?

It is doubtful if this direction resulted from a conscious decision on anyone's part. It probably just grew out of the need for something less demanding than total self-renewal. That something was the oriental idea of reincarnation.

In the Hindu religion God is conceived of as the All— pure reality and infinite Being—in fact the only Being. He, or more properly It, is called *Brahman*. The major mistake that human beings make is to think that they are indeed beings— separate individuals. The individual self, *Atman,* is in reality Brahman. The problem is that it takes a man a long time to fully realize his identity. It may require being born successively through many lifetimes before a man detaches himself from the illusion of individuality. Those furthest along on the path to God-awareness are called *Brahmins*. In other words, some people realize they are God, and some people don't; and not too much can be done for those who don't.

For many psychologically-minded people this was a welcome thought. Instead of worrying about transforming the self through strenuous mental exertion, one could just let it be. The idea was all the more convenient for those who already considered themselves high on the scale of transmigration—as most psychologically-minded people do. It was assumed that anyone who had enough interest in the first place to seek reunion with his own divine essence already possessed that union. Or to cast it into the more straightforward language of est, "You've already got It."

Some psychologists were coming to the conclusion that the self needn't be tinkered with after all: it doesn't have to be born again; it already is.

Accordingly, an elitist attitude began to appear in some quarters. In May 1980, the International Transpersonal Association announced it was setting up a "Spiritual Emergency Network," but hastened to add that nonadepts need not apply: "In order for a person to be considered by the network, there would have to be a significant spiritual emphasis in the person's unusual states of consciousness (e.g., symptoms of Kundalini awakening, experiences of death and (re)birth, past incarnation memories, archetypal phenomena, elements of extrasensory perception . . . and other forms of transpersonal experience)." The Transpersonal Association had little interest in healing the hoi polloi.

TOTAL RESPONSIBILITY

But there was more than elitism in the air. My brush with the Brahmins in the Bahamas suggests that this "new" philosophy had an old corollary—the denial of social responsibility. If I am totally responsible for my present condition, then it follows that others are totally responsible for theirs. That is the law of *karma*.

Self-awareness had already obscured other-awareness in the human potential and self-help movements. The self-awareness promoters were not only silent on social issues; they seemed unaware that humans acted in a social context. It seems not to have occurred to them that some people had neither the leisure nor the money nor the freedom from commitment that their brands of self-actualization required. For those who are tired of the same old rut, David Viscott, a successful self-help adviser, recommends the following: "Maybe it's time to buy a small farm and raise cattle. Maybe you want to move to the southern coast of Spain, and spend your days fishing or making films. Perhaps you want that small inn in the country so you can act as cook and waiter, bartender and storyteller." The typical problems depicted by self-help writers are the problems of people with American Express cards, Volvos, and Master's degrees in business or the creative arts. That a lack of money might, for some people, pose a more serious problem than a lack of self-awareness seemed outside their range of comprehension. It needed only a push from the East to carry this self-absorption to its logical conclusion.

"Being Hindu," as one critic of the East, herself an Indian, says, "means never having to say you're sorry." Psychology's recent adoption of the law of *karma* amounts to nothing less than the abandonment of social improvement. The doctrine that left the Indian caste system unchanged for centuries has become the darling of the Third Force. Anyone who cares to browse through *Profound Simplicity* or similar tracts may read the signs of the times: "The choice principle implies that social minorities are oppressed only if they allow themselves to be put in a position they call oppression." Or as the Bahamian Brahmin put it in referring to the hypothetical crippled girl, "She's only getting what she deserves."

TOWARDS THE SPIRITUAL RIGHT WING

The evidence is that a move to the spiritual right is afoot in some sectors of psychology as more and more take up the est marching slogan, "you are only responsible for your own life"—a slogan of both individual advancement and social retreat. Characteristically the psychologists sought a theological justification for this direction: they looked up and found Brahman beaming down at them. But that, of course, is an impoverished Western metaphor. More accurately, they looked inside and found total Being. They discovered a convenient fact: the Eastern religions, despite their appeal to the liberal imagination, actually provide an excellent rationale for the status quo. Turning East is not at all incompatible with turning right.

All this was already implicit in psychology's earlier kinship with certain forms of Protestantism. As I suggested previously, humanistic psychology was originally imbued with an evangelical fervor. It is remarkable to note how many prominent psychologists are the sons of ministers and how many others switched to psychology from the seminary. Although they may have lost their faith, they kept the desire to provide a born-again experience to their followers. Moreover, many of the strands that appeared in American Protestantism—revivalism, mind cure, positive thinking—also cropped up in humanistic psychology. It was to be expected, then, that it would be faced with the same temptations. It was always a temptation to the Protestant mind to turn away from social concerns and drift in one of two directions: either into individual piety, or off on a cloud of Divine Mind. The standing complaint against the evangelicals was, and is, that in their pursuit of religious experience they had forgotten the biblical command to feed the hungry. The same complaint was lodged against the mind-healers and the positive thinkers. This was the temptation, but it was vigorously resisted in most quarters of Protestantism. Christians, after all, were supposed to model themselves on a personal Savior who took a personal interest in his people. Protestantism contained no theological justification for just-let-it-be.

Humanistic psychology, too, resisted for a while the temptation to turn wholly inward, but fervor alone does not sustain a faith. While retaining some of the Christian impulse, it had abandoned all of the Christian core. There was no anchor outside the self, no one to call the self to account.

Eventually the lure of deeper self-exploration proved irresistible. While keeping one foot planted in its Protestant-American homeland, psychology leaned out to dip the other toe into the pool of ancient wisdom. The East seemed to provide the desired blend of positive thinking (you chose your destiny) and mystical shedding of responsibility (just-let-it-be) that the West could not or would not. Here there was no problem of living up to the expectations of a personal God. Brahman was purely impersonal.

So let the little crippled girls of the world stand on their own two feet, or let them at least try to pull themselves up by their own brace straps. Not all of the psychological society had arrived at that conclusion by the early 1980s—not by any means. But all the implications were there.

4

On
Serving
Two
Masters

"**I** t ought to be the oldest things that are taught to the youngest people," wrote Chesterton in 1910. The child, he complained, is oftentimes older than the theory he is taught, so that "the flopping infant of four actually has more experience . . . than the dogma to which he is made to submit."[1]

EDUCATIONAL FADS ADOPTED
WITHOUT PROPER SCRUTINY

A current illustration of this upside-down approach can be found in Catholic religious education— the last place, we might add, where Chesterton would have expected to see it. For often the youngest things are taught to the youngest people, and it is done with the aid of the youngest techniques. "Cranks and experiments," said Chesterton, "go straight to the schoolroom when they have never passed through the Parliament, the public house, the private house, the Church, or the market place."[2] Nowadays, it seems, the most recent developments in biblical criticism or the latest speculations of Dutch theologians go straight to the C.C.D. class without having to pass through the Vatican, the Magisterium, the local parish, or the Catholic or other Christian household.

The most striking example of this process is the use of

---

[1] *What's Wrong with the World?* (New York: Dodd Mead, 1910; Sheed and Ward, 1942), p. 213.
[2] *Ibid.*

contemporary psychology in Catholic education programs. The psychology of choice among Catholic educators is humanistic psychology and its various spinoffs, such as values clarification. Humanistic psychology is a prime illustration of one of those experiments that hops from the drawing board onto the blackboard without any intervening period of public trial. Catholic educators certainly didn't wait. Even before Carl Rogers, the dean of humanistic psychologists, had published his *Freedom to Learn* in 1969, he had been invited into Catholic school systems to test his innovative techniques. And religious studies textbooks, such as the Winston series, were already based on the humanistic model. In addition, almost as soon as the idea of encounter had sprouted on the American scene, it was transplanted into convents, seminaries, and high school retreats.

WEAKNESSES OF HUMANISTIC PSYCHOLOGY REVEALED

For a while, humanistic psychology did lead a charmed life. It received little initial criticism either from religious or secular circles and quickly came to be accepted as common wisdom among college-educated people. But that honeymoon period is over. Humanistic psychology looks more and more like one of those seemingly benign drugs whose harmful effects don't become apparent until years later. This is the way it now looks to many people within psychology itself who question the validity of humanistic assumptions, and who are further embarrassed by the occult leanings of prominent humanistic psychologists (Carl Rogers and Elizabeth Kubler-Ross, for instance, claim to have contacted spirits). This is the way it looks also to a growing number of educators, historians, social critics, philosophers, and ethicians, not to mention parents and public house regulars. One of the reasons criticism was late in coming is that many of the people who ought to have been involved—such as parents and, in some cases, school board members—simply had no idea that the new psychology had become so firmly emplaced in schools. When they did find out, they often raised a furor. This was the case in the well-publicized conflict that occurred over values clarification in 1979 in the Spencer-Van Etten school system near Ithaca, New York. The concern focused not only on the possibility that values clarification might be undermining traditional family values, but also on the fact that the very concept of values clarification was only a few years old at the time it was introduced into the system. Moreover, no conclusive evidence of the effectiveness of the approach was available.[3]

RELIGIOUS EDUCATION'S ROMANCE WITH KOHLBERG

Catholic religious educators, however, perhaps unaware of these criticisms, maintained or increased their holdings in humanistic psychology while better informed investors were selling off. In 1978, the first systematic appraisal of values clarification appeared in the *Review of Educational Research* with findings that contradicted the claims of values clarification proponents.[4] In 1979, however, Benziger Publishers offered a section on values clarification in Book 8 of its religious education series.[5] Both Benziger and Sadlier (the largest publisher of Catholic religious texts in America) as well as other companies had already appropriated psychologist Lawrence Kohlberg's moral development scheme for use as the most relevant way to talk about moral

---

[3] Martin Eger, "The Conflict in Moral Education: An Informal Case Study," *The Public Interest* 63 (Spring 1981), pp. 62-80.

[4] Alan Lockwood, "The Effects of Values Clarification and Moral Development Curricula on School-age Subjects: A Critical Review of Recent Research, "*Review of Educational Research* 48 No. 3 (Summer 1978).

[5] Rev. G. P. Weber, Rev. J. J. Kilgallon, and Sr. M. M. O'Shaughnessey, *Seek and Find* (Encino, CA: Benziger, 1979), pp. 81, 82.

issues. Kohlberg's work went back to the early sixties and was supported by considerable research. Moreover, his moral reasoning approach had links with respectable traditions within psychology and philosophy. But by the middle seventies Kohlberg's method was hurting from repeated blows delivered by professional psychologists and philosophers unconvinced that morality lay purely in the cognitive realm. Then came Alasdair MacIntyre's 1981 book *After Virtue,* which called into question the whole philosophical basis for the moral reasoning approach. Yet despite these developments, Benziger continued to publish a parent guide which proclaimed without qualification that "The conclusions of Kohlberg apply in the case of all human growth."[6]

Human potential psychology seemed the most relevant thing on the horizon in the midsixties. It no longer does. Secular educators tend to smile ruefully about it now as though it were one of those adolescent phases one goes through on the way to maturity. But for religious educators, humanistic psychology continues to appeal. Its themes and goals seem readily adaptable to Christian purposes. As Hamlet reminds us, however, "seems" is not the same as "is." A closer examination of humanistic psychology reveals a belief system that is in several important respects incompatible with Christian belief. This incompatibility exists on two levels: the first is incompatibility of content, the second is incompatibility of method.

CATHOLICISM AND HUMANISTIC PSYCHOLOGY: SUPERFICIAL SIMILARITIES

Much of the content of humanistic psychology derives from the central assumption that man is good and has no inclination

---

[6] Rev. G. P. Weber, Rev. J. J. Kilgallon, *Growth in Peace: Parent Guide* (Encino, CA: Benziger, 1975), p. 26.

toward evil. Selfishness, aggression, and other undesirable behaviors are blamed on man's environment, not on man himself. The biblical notion that man is weakened by sin is either implicitly or explicitly rejected by most psychologists of this persuasion. Erich Fromm, for example, states that his psychology would be untenable if the doctrine of original sin were true.

Unlike the Christian view, the psychological one fails to distinguish between physical or existential goodness and moral goodness. Man is simply good as he is. As a consequence, much stress is laid on simply being oneself and accepting oneself. This self-acceptance is encouraged without regard to any prior transformation of the self, meaning, of course, that the need for repentance, for forgiveness, for baptism, or for God's grace are all nullified at the outset. Tied in with this concept is the standard humanist notion that man is perfectible and can achieve this perfectibility through his own powers. In the language of human potential psychology, people are either "self-actualized," or "self-determined," or "self-fulfilled."[7]

THE CROSS IS RENDERED UNINTELLIGIBLE

This very broad broom sweeps away a few more Catholic/ Christian dogmas. Since man can perfect himself without God's help, and since there is very little wrong with him in the first place, Christ's sacrifice on the cross becomes both unnecessary and unintelligible. Sacraments, likewise, are rendered unnecessary as means of grace, and come instead to be looked upon merely as celebrations of human virtue. Prayer also becomes an activity of dubious merit within this framework. And the Christian practices of self-denial and sacrifice can only appear as

---

[7] Abraham Maslow, *The Farther Reaches of Human Nature* (New York: Viking Press, 1971), p. 7.

obstacles to growth. In humanistic psychology man achieves fulfillment by satisfying his wants, not by denying them. Other Christian virtues such as obedience and conformity to God's will are difficult to reconcile with the humanistic emphasis on self-will and autonomy. Where the psychological model prevails, these virtues will tend to be slighted or ignored even by Christian educators.

OBJECTIVITY OF TRUTH DENIED

Another stock ingredient in humanistic psychology is subjectivism. The idea of a common truth to which all are bound is seen as an encroachment on freedom. Hence, the only truths are personal truths. This attitude explains why humanistic therapies are invariably nonjudgmental, and why humanistic education is geared in the direction of having students create their own values. Moreover, since the humanist has no objective criteria for choosing values, he has to rely on instincts. "When an activity *feels* as though it is valuable or worthwhile," writes Rogers, "it *is* worth doing."[8]

All of this is, of course, very much in keeping with modern sentiments, but it is difficult to square with Catholic and Protestant belief which maintains that truth is both objective and unchanging, and that the most important truths (the Trinity, the Incarnation, the Redemption) come to us through divine revelation rather than self-revelation.[9]

---

[8]Carl Rogers, *On Becoming a Person* (Boston: Houghton Mifflin, 1961), pp. 90, 91.

[9] Of course, Catholic tradition also maintains that there is a natural revelation which reveals to us the existence of God as well as the existence of a natural moral order. Because of this natural revelation, St. Paul preached that those pagans who practiced immorality were without excuse. In this sense, honest insight or self-awareness will lead us to a knowledge of truth, though not all truths.

A glance at the careers of the most prominent humanistic psychologists shows an almost invariable progression from these subjectivist principles to an embrace with Eastern and immanentist modes of thought. Why Catholic teachers should want to follow along this path is a puzzle. One can only suppose they have been attracted to humanistic psychology because of certain surface similarities to Christianity. The talk about loving, sharing, and caring sound Christian. So does the humanistic admonition against making judgments, and the humanistic concern for the little child within us. Ideas about wholeness and freedom and values seem to echo Christian sentiments as well. And "the dignity of the person" is high on the list of humanistic priorities, just as it is with Christians. Still, the basic principles of humanistic psychology cannot always be synthesized with basic Christian belief; efforts to mix the two will generally lead to confusion.

THE GOOD NEWS IS REDUCED TO NICE NEWS

Examples of this confusion abound in current religious texts. Book One of the Benziger series answers the question, "Who am I?" by saying, "I am me. There are things I can do and say. See the gifts I have. I am me. I can talk and run and hug. I am special."[10] In fact, "All boys and girls are good and special."[11] Book Four states that Jesus ". . . was trying to show (people) how they could be themselves." In the same book, children are told "you must like yourself for what you are. . . ."[12] Book Eight reminds us that "A person has value by the very fact of being human. A person, a 'you,' has rights, needs and worth indepen-

---

[10] Rev. Gerard Weber, *In Christ Jesus* (Encinco, CA: Benziger, 1981), pp. 90, 91.

[11] *Ibid.*

[12] *Ibid.*, Book Four, p. 40.

dent of other people." Consequently, "knowing yourself through self-examination can help develop your self-esteem."[13] By implication, poor self-esteem means you simply haven't taken stock of your abilities.

These sentiments are mixed in with genuine Christian doctrine, but one wonders why they are there at all. In the first place, students are going to pick up the idea of self-esteem from a dozen other sources. In the second place, the constant harping on the theme tends to reduce the Good News to the status of nice news because of the implied suggestion that there was never any bad news about the human condition to begin with.

SELF-REVELATION VS. DIVINE REVELATION

The writers of these texts themselves seem confused, bound as they are on the one hand to Christian belief, and on the other to the psychological faith. Thus, in Book Seven of Benziger: "We aim at becoming our true self, what we are capable of becoming, the person God and nature intended us to be. We strive to become the person *we* want to be. . . ."[14]

It is not at all clear in this passage whether we should become what God intends us to be or what we want to be, or whether the two are always to be equated. The emphasis on the "we," however, along with all the earlier encouragements to self-esteem and self-determination, suggests that what *we* want will do just fine.

There is a similar problem in Book Eight where we are told that "Saint Paul had self-esteem and that this particular self-

---

[13] Weber, et al., *Seek and Find,* pp. 118, 92.
[14] Rev. Gerald Weber, et al., *Think and Serve* (Encino, CA: Benziger, 1979), p. 41.

knowledge helped him in his mission to spread Christ to all people."[15] Then follows the story of Paul's conversion, but the whole thing is forced into the procrustean bed of a self-esteem format. The point of it is not that Paul came to know God, but that "Paul came to know himself through God"—as though knowing oneself was the be-all and end-all of existence.[16]

This attempt to assimilate the New Testament to the categories of psychology results, predictably, in a distortion. The Benziger book states that Paul's "journey toward self-knowledge took a lifetime," but this is very nearly the reverse of the truth.[17] If there is one story in the annals of mankind that is *not* about the gradual acquisition of self-knowledge, it is the story of Paul's conversion. In fact, it is not primarily about self-knowledge at all.

SEXUAL MORALITY UNDERMINED

This kind of double message—the presentation of a Christian theme along with a psychological one which tends to undo it—is particularly apparent in the treatment of marriage and sexuality. On the one hand, a typical text will say that sex is to be reserved for marriage, which is a sacrament. On the other hand, the next chapter may very well present a section on "What young men should know about young women in lovemaking" followed by "What young women should know about young men in love-making."[18]

---

[15] Weber, et al., *Seek and Find,* p. 92.
[16] *Ibid.,* p. 99.
[17] *Ibid.*
[18] Ronald J. Wilkins and Nancy B. Wilkins, *Man and Woman: A Christian Perspective on Human Sexuality, Love and Marriage* (Dubuque, IA: William C. Brown, 1980), pp. 96-105.

For some reason, these young men and women who are supposed to be waiting for marriage need to know the facts about arousal (there are three stages), tempo, and style, and about "the inability of some men to control the ejaculatory aspect of sexual excitement," which is "one of the principal reasons for the disappointment young women feel in premarital experimentation."[19] Young people should remember however, that "sexual intercourse outside of marriage is considered less than psychologically wise."[20]

An extreme example of the confusion present in many of the newer texts is the treatment of marriage in the *Conscience and Concern* series published by Holt, Rinehart, and Winston. About four-fifths of the chapter on marriage consists of a lengthy excerpt (three pages of double columns) from Carl Rogers's book *Becoming Partners: Marriage and Its Alternatives*.

Now, anyone familiar with Rogers's work knows that he is far more committed to the idea of change than he is to the idea of marriage. This particular excerpt ends with Rogers commenting on his own marriage: "We have *grown* as individuals and in the process we have grown together."[21] Yet elsewhere in *Becoming Partners* Rogers makes it plain that it is just as acceptable for couples to grow apart: the governing priority is growth, not fidelity. Perhaps a more pointed commentary, however, may be made on the fact that this same chapter devotes only two lines to Christ's views on marriage. When you attempt to serve two masters, one of them will not be served very well.

A further consequence of the infatuation with human potentialism is omission of crucial content. Christian doctrines

---

[19] *Ibid.*, p. 103.
[20] *Ibid.*, p. 99.
[21] Eileen D. Mimoso, *Sacraments: Signs of Community, Conscience and Concern Series* (Minneapolis: Winston Press, 1974), p. 39.

which do not lend themselves to the humanistic framework are partially presented or simply omitted. As a result, the content of these books reveals very little about man's sinfulness and quite a lot about man's goodness; very little about grace and quite a lot about deserved reward; very little about Hell and very little about Heaven. Time and again, the fullness of doctrinal belief is distorted through emphasizing those beliefs which are in keeping with the humanistic tenets—man is good; man is deserving; man is autonomous; man is the measure of all things.

The habit of omitting or slighting crucial Christian doctrine even extends to the illustrations. Although all of the psychologically based texts are heavily illustrated, there are surprisingly few depictions of the crucifixion. Book Seven of the Benziger Series is over three hundred pages in length with at least that many illustrations and photographs; yet there is only one picture of Christ on the cross. Book Eight, with an equal number of illustrations, has no crucifixion scene. Neither do Books Six, Five, Four, or Three. Of eight books in the Sadlier series, only three have crucifixion scenes.[22] The vision of Christ hanging on the cross for our sins—the central symbol of the Christian faith—is apparently out of line with the humanistic emphasis on our goodness.

PREOCCUPATION WITH "GROWTH"

When supernatural or nonhumanistic topic *are* covered, they are given a curious slant. Sin, for instance, is usually treated as an impediment to growth—not to growth in Christ, just to growth. For example, God's message to Cain as rendered by Benziger is, "You can grow; you can become a better and wiser

---

[22] *The Lord of Life Series* (New York: Sadlier, 1979).

person."[23] Accordingly, penance is viewed as a challenge to self-understanding, a chance to talk on an "I-you level with the priest about ourselves."[24] But penance is not the remedy of choice in these books. Rather, the emphasis in book after book is on values clarification, or Kohlberg's stages of moral growth, or on some form of decision-making.

Chapter One of *Understanding Christian Morality,* in the William C. Brown series, presents Kohlberg's six stages as though they were scientific fact.[25] Benziger, on the other hand, prescribes the seven steps of values clarification. Step One asks, "Does my position make me *feel good?*"[26] As is so often true in these texts, this emphasis follows not from any Christian principles, but from psychological premises—in this case, the assumption that wrongdoing is simply a matter of poor decision-making skills. Good decision-making is apparently almost the whole point of the Gospels, which are "a help to Christians in making their decisions because they show Jesus and the others accepting both *challenge* and the *familiar* as part of their decision-making process."[27]

THE DALE CARNEGIE APPROACH TO SPIRITUALITY

Another method for firming up the self is positive thinking. One of the earlier Sadlier books tells the story of Olympic skier Jill Kinmont, who was paralyzed in an accident, and how she "be-

---

[23] Weber, et al., *Think and Serve,* p. 70.
[24] Weber, et al., *Seek and Find,* p. 254.
[25] Ronald J. Wilkins, *Understanding Christian Morality* (Dubuque, IA: William C. Brown, 1982), pp. 9-12.
[26] Weber, et al., *Seek and Find,* pp. 81, 82.
[27] *Ibid.,* p. 287.

gan to believe in herself once more."[28] In a subsequent chapter, an attempt is made to relate her tragedy to the Fall, and her new hope to the new hope we have because of Christ. But it is difficult to correct the impression given in the earlier chapter that obstacles are overcome simply by tapping deep inner resources, or that the worst thing about obstacles is that they "threaten our image of ourselves."[29] Kinmont's recovery is made possible by the intervention of a friend, but also because "She had her identity: Jill Kinmont, a person with a lot to live for and a lot to give others."[30]

The positive thinking theme is much more explicit in *The Fully Alive Experience,* a retreat workbook for high school students. Chapter Two starts off with this quote from William James:

> The greatest discovery in our generation is that human beings, by changing the inner attitudes of their minds, can change the outer aspects of their lives.[31]

The right "inner attitude" comes from "choosing or deciding to esteem ourselves."[32] A few paragraphs later, the student is advised: "Through countering, modeling, stretching and praying, we can come to a life-giving self-image."[33] Life-giving self-image" is, of course, a new star in the Catholic firmament. Readers of this religious self-help manual may be forgiven if they conclude that salvation is something you do for yourself.

———————

[28] Msgr. John F. Barry, *One Faith, One Lord* (New York: Sadlier, 1976), pp. 12, 13.

[29] *Ibid.,* p. 14.

[30] *Ibid.,* p. 13.

[31] John Powell, S.J. and Loretto Brady, *The Fully Alive Experience* (Allen, TX: Argus Communications, 1980), Chap. 2, p. 1.

[32] *Ibid.,* Chap. 3, p. 1.

[33] *Ibid.*

PROBLEMS WITH METHODOLOGY

The content of the textbooks, however, may be only a partial indicator of the depth of the psychological mentality that exists in religious education classrooms. The publishers still want an *Imprimatur* or *Nihil Obstat,* and this desire insures that the emphasis on personal growth will be balanced by doctrinal content. The teachers, however, are much freer in this regard; casual observation suggests that they lean even more heavily toward psychology than do the textbooks.

One teacher, when asked to explain the doctrinal content of her course, replied, "We are teaching the children to grow, to become whole persons, to question, to choose values." Another answered, "We are showing them how to become whole persons."

An informal survey by the authors of this article indicates that these responses are representative of the agenda on the mind of the new breed of religious educator. But even if the teachers and the textbooks were doctrinally sound, there would remain the question of method. While all of the newer texts do present basic Catholic beliefs, there is often a problem with the manner in which they are presented. The major problem has to do with the humanistic emphasis on truth as a personal construct, independent of objective norms.

REVEALED TRUTHS VS. REVEALED OPINIONS

The Church has always claimed to deal in revealed truths, not revealed opinions. The textbook writers are aware of this, of course, and make gestures in the direction of asserting Catholic doctrine as infallible truth. At several points in all of these texts, there are conscious attempts to inform the student that he can't simply make up his own truths whenever he wants to. The authors seem to realize that this is the direction toward which humanistic psychology leads. Yet, it is a temptation they themselves can't resist. For example, in the Sadlier book *One Faith, One Lord* the student is invited to decide upon the powers of God himself:

> Take a stand on what you believe by choosing one of the answers below. In the column on the right, give the reasons for your choice.

Among the choices given are:

1. "I believe God created the universe."
2. "I believe God had nothing to do with creation."[34]

This is from a section at the back of most Sadlier chapters entitled "What It Means to Me." Likewise, most chapters in the later Benziger books end with an invitation for students to write down a definition of this or that Catholic doctrine "in your own words." In the *Conscience and Concern* series, students are asked:

> Do you agree or disagree that the sacraments are celebrations of important moments in a person's life? Why?

> From your point of view, what is the future of each of the sacraments?[35]

Similar questions of opinion can be found in many of these modern religious texts. Questions asking if premarital sex is permissible, if religion is valuable, or if attendance at Sunday Mass is important are often presented to readers as matters of choice. In one of the William C. Brown books students are

---

[34] Barry, *One Faith, One Lord,* p. 10.
[35] Mimoso, *Sacraments: Signs of Community,* p. 55.

asked, "Do you think that abortion is a moral solution to an unwanted pregnancy?" and on the same page, "Write a short paragraph giving your philosophy of life."[36]

This "you decide" approach to the faith is dictated by the schizoid nature of the textbook writers' belief. Their double allegiance to Catholicism on the one hand and to a self-oriented psychology on the other guarantees that every advance on the doctrinal front is canceled out by a concession to solipsism. It is an unfortunate illustration of the old adage that how you teach is more important than what you teach.

In *Catechesi Tradendae,* John Paul II states: "A technique is of value in catechesis only to the extent that it serves the faith that is to be transmitted and learned; otherwise, it is of no value."[37] It is difficult to see how the techniques mentioned above serve the Catholic faith. At best, the student will merely be confused by these double messages. More likely, he will be misled into supposing that God's laws are arbitrary and Catholic morality relative. The (hopefully) unintended message is that Church teachings are wide open to subjective interpretation, and with that comes the implication that the authority of the Church to pronounce on matters of right and wrong is no different from that of any other authority—indeed, no better than personal authority.

THE HIDDEN AGENDA

All of which leads to another point. Educators often speak of a hidden curriculum in the schools—values which are not explicit-

---

[36] Wilkins, *Understanding Christian Morality,* p. 107.
[37] Pope John Paul II, *Catechesi Tradendae* (Boston: Daughters of St. Paul, 1979), p. 48.

ly stated, but are subtly conveyed by actions and priorities. The hidden curriculum in the psychologically inspired texts looks very much like some form of secular humanism. The penchant for psychologizing is, of course, the most obvious example of it. The repeated use of identity quizzes (on a computer card format), self-esteem tests, personality profiles, values inventories, and relationship compatibility tests suggests that Christian growth is to be measured in terms of human fulfillment.

But the secular tone is not by any means limited to psychology. The Sadlier series, for instance, makes much ado about Arthur Fonzarelli, Archie Bunker, Mary Tyler Moore, and other media celebrities, and juxtaposes their photos with pictures of Apostles and Martyrs.[38] Other series specialize in the use of photo illustrations that can only be described as contemporary-mod. The intent here is either to speak to the students' interests or to show that Christianity is relevant to the modern world. The effect, however, is to ratify secular culture and place it on an even footing with Christianity.

CHURCH PRESENTED AS A MERELY PIOUS ACCESSORY

Christians are, at times, supposed to separate themselves from the world and even to judge it. But it is difficult to see how these texts, even with their stress on autonomous judgment, could encourage that kind of Christianity. Although much emphasis is laid on community in these texts, one does not get the sense that that community is the City of God. It looks instead like the secular city with an overlay of religious sentiment. The Catholic Church appears no different from any other socially aware organization or movement. If it is made to seem relevant,

---

[38] See particularly Barry, *One Faith, One Lord,* pp. 29, 44.

it is also made to seem superfluous—a pious accessory that one might choose to complement one's existing repertoire of secular ideas.

It is not that the sacred element has been excluded—the Benziger series, for example, is replete with Bible stories—but that it has been severely compromised by the tone of sunny rationalism which pervades these texts. The constant reference to "communications breakdowns," "risk-taking," "involvement," "decision-making," "personhood," "I-you relationships," "getting in touch," "self-disclosure," "awareness," and "assertiveness" carries the implication that all the deep mysteries of faith can be encompassed in secular/psychological categories. In fact, there is very little sense that there are *any* deep mysteries—that there might be elements of the faith so awesome and unfathomable that they exist far beyond the reach of the social sciences.

GOSPELS TRIVIALIZED

Even Christ is reduced to size. "In His life," according to one text, "Jesus showed what it meant to be a whole person."[39] In another text, Christ seems to be little more than an advertisement for the telephone company: "Christ quite likely was trying to teach something about the miracle taking place every time one person reaches out and touches the life of another."[40] This type of thing, along with the juxtaposition of the sacred and the trendy, only serves to trivialize the Gospels, to set them within mundane limits. Reading these books, one gets the impression that Christianity is little more than an ethical or value system. "Here," they say in effect, "are some examples of very good

---

[39] Weber, et. al., *Seek and Find*, p. 14.
[40] Peter Russell, C.F.X., *Who Cares? Conscience and Concern Series* (Minneapolis: Holt, Rinehart & Winston, 1971), p. 46.

people with well-thought-out values. Knowing about them can help you to develop a value system of your own."

Even if it were true that psychologically based techniques for promoting values and growth did work—and that is far from certain—it would be a small gain if in the process students suffered a loss of the sacred. Almost everything else in today's world conspires to rob young people of what Wordsworth called the "vision splendid"—the child's intuitive sense of wonder. The Church has always stood on the side of the child in this matter, and proclaimed that the world is indeed uncanny and marvelous, with greater marvels to come. Against any number of temptations, she has not allowed the light of revelation to "fade into the light of common day."

But the current attraction which some Catholic educators have for humanistic psychology must be seen as just such a temptation. The temptation is understandable, of course. It is a fine thing to be a whole person. But it is better to enter the Kingdom of Heaven maimed than to enter the other place brimming with psychological completeness. And better still to remember that there are far greater visions in Christianity than the vision of the whole person.

THE SENSE OF SACREDNESS MUST BE RESTORED

The irony of all this is that Catholic education was psychologically far more sophisticated in the past than it is today.

Catholic educators knew how to evoke responses from regions of the psyche that lie far deeper than those surface areas given over to concerns of decision-making and self-concept. That this is so is attested by the almost indelible nature Catholicism once had. You could no more get rid of it than you could escape the color of your skin.

That does not appear to be the case today. Catholicism is rather easily shucked off by many. And one reason, certainly, is that an inferior brand of psychology has insinuated itself into the catechetical movement. While humanistic psychology may be helpful in some areas (such as therapy), it cannot be freely applied to all areas or in all circumstances. Sometimes it simply won't work. It is an inappropriate tool.

Anyone trained in pedagogy knows that each subject area has its own appropriate methods. A technique that is appropriate for a creative writing class may not be at all useful in a physics class. And a gym instructor will not want to use the same methods as the social studies teacher or the school counselor.

Now in many respects teaching Catholic/Christian faith is more like teaching a physics class than a social studies class. It has to do with immutable laws. One does not decide upon the validity of divine truths by the group discussion method any more than one uses that method to decide upon the point at which water boils.

In other respects, teaching Christianity is like teaching poetry or folklore or myth. Memorization—the storing up of wisdom—is called for. In still other respects, it is like a class in gym or dance: the muscles need to be trained as well as the mind; the proper movements and steps have to be practiced over and over.

But finally, of course, the faith is literally like nothing else on earth. The church is at once our supernatural mother and the Bride of Christ, and God our Father dwells in unapproachable light. These mysteries can only be approached in an atmosphere of reverence and humility. The atmosphere of free inquiry and self-concern simply won't work.

All of this was understood once. It represents an older form of psychology—what was once referred to as "the psychology of the soul." But it is precisely by these oldest ways, if we may extend Chesterton's observation, that the youngest people ought to be taught.

5
Why the Secular Needs the Sacred

A t the time of the U.S. Supreme Court's deliberations over the legality of Christmas crèche displays, ABC's "Nightline" interviewed, among others, Father Robert Drinan and the mayor of Pawtucket, Rhode Island, the city where the issue first boiled over onto the national scene.

Predictably, Father Drinan worried about the trauma and mental anguish such displays cause to little boys and girls who are not Christian. It was a case, said he, of the arrogant majority imposing its values on a minority, and it shouldn't be allowed to happen in a pluralistic society. The mayor of Pawtucket, on the other hand, was in favor of a Christmas display, but took pains to downplay its religious nature. The manger scene, he said, had become a tradition in Pawtucket, and people should be allowed to keep their traditions. If you look at it in the right way, suggested the mayor, it's not really a church/state problem at all.

It's understandable that he would take such a tack. This *is* a pluralistic society, after all. And indeed his argument is quite typical. Many attempts at defending the "church" side of church/state issues are framed in similar terms. It's either a defense ("we're not really trying to influence anyone else") or a demand ("Christians have a right to educate their children in their own way"). Unfortunately, neither approach gets at the main source of resistance to the religious side of such questions, because the main problem is not hostility toward religious practices (though there is plenty of that) but indifference. A great many people have come to the conclusion that as far as the everyday functioning of society is concerned, religion doesn't matter one way or the other. So why rock the boat? In other words, there exists a widespread assumption that the secular can get along without the sacred. From this point of view, religious beliefs may be seen as nice and commendable, and even helpful, but they are not seen as necessary to leading a good life or having a good society. Many Americans seem to believe that a secular culture can maintain morality without a sacred core. And so, if a Christmas scene offends, it's better to pluck it out and replace it with a nonoffensive Santa. If the crèche is nothing more than a nice tradition, it's not worth the fuss.

The mayor might have had more effect on this indifferent mass if he had said what he probably really thinks: cut out the crèche and you cut out the heart of Western civilization. And he would be right. The sacred view of life is not simply an alternative within society; it is indispensable to society. To step away from it is to step into the void.

What does the sacred do for the state? The brief answer is simply that it makes sense out of life—a service the state cannot perform for itself, and yet without which it cannot exist.

This is hardly a new argument, but it is one that is not often used. Although it can be sensed or intuited by the simplest folk, it cannot be easily put into words. Nevertheless, it's worth trying. Dostoyevsky puts the matter in its most direct formulation when he has Ivan Karamazov say: "If there is no God everything is permissible." Dostoyevsky meant this not as a figure of speech, but as something akin to a mathematical axiom, something along the lines of "if a triangle has one right or obtuse angle, its other two angles must be acute."

FIXITY AND FORMLESSNESS

It is instructive to note that when scholars try to describe the idea of the sacred, they do, in fact, tend to talk in precise geometrical terms rather than in vague spiritual ones. In *The Sacred and the Profane* Mircea Eliade returns again and again to the idea that the sacred is the fixed point without which no orientation can be established. The sacred "fixes the limits" and "establishes order" in what is otherwise a formless and chaotic fluidity or relativity. Ordinary things and events only derive their meaning from their relationship to the sacred order. On any other view than a sacred one, reality reduces to a chance combination of matter; and values, likewise, are reduced to the status of arbitrary choices since there is nothing fixed against which they can be measured. On that view there is no arguing with Ivan Karamazov or, for that matter, with Adolf Hitler who also said "everything is permitted."

The secular attitude has it that morality is a basically rational construct requiring no reference to a sacred or religious dimension. But the truth is, the profane can't get along very well without the sacred. The diminishment of the sacred and mystical does not make the rest of life seem more sensible. The result, rather, is that profane or secular life seems more senseless. The deterioration of Greek mythological religion did not clear the way for a flowering of Aristotelians so much as it brought forth a crop of cynics and sophists. The French Revolution, born of the marriage of enlightened reason and antireligious fervor, produced a reign of terror and irrationality. Nietzsche's announcement of God's demise was followed by the existentialist conclusion that life is absurd—as it is, of course, without the sacred.

This can be seen most clearly—if one is willing to look—in matters of law. Without a fixed and transcendent order everything is arbitrary. Yet few people are comfortable with that idea. Most still need a fixed system of order. And for this purpose the rule of law serves admirably. Or does it? As a people come less to believe in the gods, they come more to depend on the law. They need it more since they have no heavenly standard to which to conform their behavior. In such a society the law must be made to work overtime. Sooner or later, however, purely legal attempts to provide and maintain order are bound to fail since law itself is eventually revealed to be arbitrary. Cut off from its relationship to the supernatural order and from the natural (which is only a derivative of the former), the law can't bear a close examination. Even the dullest will eventaully see the skull beneath the skin.

In our present society this process takes many forms, but the one which touches almost everyone's life is the transformation of the relationship between adult and child, particularly at school and in the home. In both institutions there has been a substitution of legal and contractual lines of authority for natural and sacred lines of authority. This substitution has already had disastrous consequences. Here let us say a few words about these two types of authority.

TWO ORDERS OF AUTHORITY

The most direct way of sorting out these differing spheres of authority is to ask two simple questions: Where do teachers get their authority over students? Where do parents get their authority over children? Modern man does not have ready answers to these questions (my students, both undergraduate and graduate, tend to be dumbfounded when I ask them), but his ancestors did. They would simply answer that such authority was natural, or that it came from God. However imperfectly, worldly order was thought to reflect a natural order or a heavenly one. In Christendom, for example, the authority of a father over his children was thought to derive from the absolute authority of God the Father. The marriage bond was considered a reflection of the marriage of Christ and his Church. The family, in short, constituted a sacred unit. Crossing the family threshold brought one into a different order of being; so did the crossing of the Church threshold. Other religions may have had less explicit theologies supporting parental authority, but the same ideas prevailed. For example, in ancient Roman society the father had priestly duties. Parental authority was mystical authority.

Instead of speaking in terms of the supernatural origin of

66

parental authority, one can, of course, simply refer to its natural origin. Nevertheless, the import is similar. The same element of irrationality is there. At least, it would be perceived by the modern mind as irrational because, once again, the appeal is to an axiomatically fixed order. Parental authority over children derives not from some rational, mutually-satisfying agreement, but from generation. To the question, Why should it be this way? one can only reply that this is the natural order of things. There is no way to reason logically to such a conclusion because it is not a conclusion but rather one of those bedrock observations about human nature that are not the result of logic but the source of it.

Schools and teachers, by extension, also shared in this authority, because they stood *in loco parentis*. The respect due to them was similar to the respect due to one's parents. Moreover, formal schooling was almost always conducted within the precincts of church or temple. The phrase "hallowed halls of learning" once had a literal meaning.

It is true, of course, that parental authority was also legally upheld, but the law never pretended to grant that authority; it was merely recognizing an existing order, much as the law of sanctuary recognized the legitimacy of another order.

The point is that these other orders, whether they be conceived of as natural or supernatural, are in a different order from the prevailing notion of authority. What is the prevailing notion? It is a social-contract view. Authority comes from the consent of the governed. It is legitimate only so far as it conforms to certain reasonable rules freely agreed to. The most convenient model for this view of authority is the business agreement. The parties to such an agreement have decided for one reason or another that their interests are best served by a mutual compact. Once they have given their consent, they are bound by the contract. Any subsequent difficulties can be interpreted and adjudicated by a court of law.

Much of the moral confusion in our society, and much of

the weakening of traditional modes of authority, stems from the extension of this contractual order into areas which were once within the realm of the sacred or natural orders.[1] In short, Caesar's slice of the pie is larger. The law no longer stops at the church door when in pursuit of criminals, nor does it show much inclination to stop at the school door or the door to your house where other matters are concerned.

This is not to say that the line between the secular and the sacred is clearly drawn. In some ways the law still acts as though it were grounded in some sacred soil. Why else, for example, would the penalty for rape be so much more severe than that for other types of assault, especially when the actual physical injury may be slight? There seems to be a residue here of the ancient belief that the sex act partakes or ought to partake of the sacred realm, so that a violation of a woman's body is a violation of the sacred order. Another trace of the sacred realm is exhibited in the honor and deference with which judges are treated, although the logical conclusion of the rational/contractual approach would be to replace them with computers. But though government may from time to time indulge itself in shows of solemnity, it seems increasingly to demand that other institutions conform to the contractarian model.

WHAT IS AT STAKE

Many people, of course, are not overly bothered by the encroachment of the secular into sacred areas. I think this nonchalance stems in large part from a failure to see the problem clearly, because, even from a secular point of view, much is at

---

[1] For an excellent treatment of the two kinds of authority, see Joseph Sobran, *Single Issues* (New York: The Human Life Press, 1983).

stake. The problem resides in the fact that strictly rational or contractual approaches to life do not yield the harvest of rationality and harmony one might expect. Quite the contrary. One reason why this is so is that the keeping of contracts depends on qualities and virtues that do not flourish in a strictly contractual milieu. For example, parties to a contract are expected to enter into the agreement in good faith and are further expected to maintain loyalty to the spirit or intent of the agreement. But virtues such as "good faith" and "loyalty" are generated for the most part within the sacred order. If that order is extinguished, the only guarantee of a contract is fear of the law. A society which thinks it can manage on a purely secular level will find it has need of a great many policemen or a great many lawyers, or both.

Without some higher sanction, a civil society is reduced to nothing but a compact of individuals for the sake of protecting their own self-interests. And there is no compelling moral reason why an individual should stick by that compact when it is no longer in his or her interest to do so. The legal order can support and encourage morality, but it is not the source of morality. Morality originates in such irrational basic units as the family and the church. A government which wishes to maintain a moral climate among its citizens is wise not to tamper with those basic units.

And herein lies the problem. Although government still manages to wrap itself in a cloak of near divinity—the Bill of Rights and the Constitution have the force of Scripture in this country—government is slowly depriving other institutions of their claim to a separate authority derived from a fundamental order. We are moving in the direction of the idea that parents and teachers hold their authority not from sacred or natural realms but from consent, as the state does. From there it is only a short step to the next conclusion: the state has a duty to make sure that these other groups do business the way *it* does business.

From whence do parents and teachers derive their authority over children? Once the initial astonishment has passed, most of my students conclude that it must be from the state. Where else could it come from? This attitude is already widespread, and it means, of course, that the bonds between parent and child, or teacher and pupil, must be reinterpreted not in terms of blood and duty, but in terms of a compact of equals.

THE HOSTILITY BETWEEN THE GENERATIONS

This, as we are beginning to see, is a formula for disaster. Primarily it will serve to increase hostility between the generations. After all, if we are all fellow citizens, what right do you have to tell me what to do? That is the way the child or adolescent will reason. Despite the fact that schools and parents are more permissive than they have ever been, children are more restive than ever. Why shouldn't they be? They have learned that government is by consent, but they have little say in the governments that immediately concern them, those of home and school. Traditional modes of authority, once they are divorced from any concept of the sacred or natural order, will appear as arbitrary impositions of will, with the paradoxical result that children perceive even the most lenient schools and families as oppressive.

This attitude is reinforced by television, which also acts to eliminate the distinctions between children and adults. As Neil Postman points out in *The Disappearance of Childhood,* television makes it possible for everyone to see and hear the same things.[2] The programs which adults watch are the pro-

---

[2] Neil Postman, *The Disappearance of Childhood* (New York: Delacorte, 1982).

grams which children watch. In fact, producers make a conscious effort to capture as wide an age range as possible for their shows. And the amount of programming specifically for children is declining. In addition, children on television dress, talk, and act like adults. They seem wise and rational beyond their years. They are extraordinarily sophisticated about the world, and often must intervene in adult affairs to put things right. Indeed, adult problems and relationships are presented as little different from the ones children are involved in. Parental authority is not necessarily scorned in these programs, but it seems to be acceptable only so long as it is reasonable and can be explained to the satisfaction of the child as being in his own interest. The children of the media age can be forgiven if they think they are every bit equal to adults, for that is the impression conveyed by television. It is understandable that they might resent the real-life parent or teacher who doesn't accept their equality or who thinks that his own word ought to be sufficient authority. Making the child equal to his parents or teachers thus becomes an effective way of alienating his allegiance to them.

Adults, in turn, will experience increased resentment toward children. If children are simply fellow citizens rather than a sacred trust, it is difficult to see why one should sacrifice for them. It is inevitable that many adults will come to look upon them simply as burdens—state-imposed burdens at that. Parents and teachers will reason that they owe children nothing but the minimum legal requirements.

By increasing the legal rights of children, children's advocates hope, of course, to better protect them. But a child needs more than legal protection; he needs love as well. Turning family matters into civil-rights issues is a formula for insuring that he won't get it. Consider a proposal for licensing parents by the state which appeared in *Philosophy and Public Affairs*. The author, Hugh LaFollette, sees this as necessary for the protection of children, but also for the purpose of destroying the idea of parents' "natural sovereignty."[3] It would certainly have the latter effect, but would it have the former? Would it really protect children? Once you destroy the idea of natural sovereignty, you also destroy the notion that children owe any particular honor, respect, or obedience to their mothers and fathers. It would be an unusual adult who could suffer such an arrangement without eventually resorting to indifference, neglect, or even physical abuse. The only thing the child will be protected from is his parents' love. These considerations help to explain why the proposed "squeal rule" (requiring that parents be notified when their minor children seek contraceptives) is such a sensitive issue. Those who oppose the rule—who usually also favor laws allowing minors to obtain abortions without parental consent—are saying in effect to parents: This is none of your business; this is a matter between your child and *his* federally-funded agency. But if they are right, it is difficult to imagine in what areas parents might still retain hegemony, since this one lies so close to the center of family life.

THE SCHOOLS: MORAL AUTHORITY AND LEGAL AUTHORITY

A similar subversion of traditional authority goes on in schools. And with it goes the same recipe for hostility. Edward Wynne, writing in *The Public Interest,* demonstrates in very concrete ways how court decisions concerning student rights force educators to abdicate their parental duties and become instead "mere custodians."[4] Such decisions as *Tinker v. Des Moines, Goss v.*

---

[3] Quoted in Bruce A. Miller, "Student Advocates, Teachers' Rights," *American Educator,* Spring 1981.

[4] Edward A. Wynne, "What are the Courts doing to Our Children?" *The Public Interest,* Summer 1981, pp. 3-18.

Lopez, and *Wood v. Strickland* helped create an air of uncertainty and confusion among educators. In one school, writes Wynne, a principal is advised by the school lawyer not to interfere with a student who wears a "Marijuana" stenciled T-shirt. In another district, school board members are advised to avoid written discipline codes lest these be used as a basis for litigation. (However, in the Boston schools, students receive a booklet each September informing them of their rights and legal recourses.) In another school a security guard is uncertain about his right to search a student he suspects of holding drugs. The student (who actually is holding drugs) gets away with it. The guard feels humiliated.[5]

The upshot of all this, observes Wynne, is that schools become more depersonalized, less communal, less familial. Teachers become more hostile or indifferent, retreating from the kind of engagement and concern that was possible under the aegis of *in loco parentis.* In addition to losing the power to discipline, they lose the power to care. Their attitude becomes that of the civil servant or bureaucrat toward the clients he must serve. In both school and home, the result of a real or perceived equality for children is a mutual withdrawal of loyalty and love. Without those virtues, obedience to rules is secured only by fear and by force, which in concrete terms means that we will have more battered children as well as more battered parents, more social workers to be a watchdog over families, and more security guards to police the schools.

That it doesn't *have* to be this way is attested by the success of parochial schools in some of the most unpromising areas of our cities. Children not only behave better in these schools; they are happier in them. In addition, school spirit is

---

[5] *Ibid.*

73

higher, and so is parental involvement. Of course, the difference between public and parochial schools can be explained away by many sociological factors, but one must eventually contend with a nonsociological fact: parochial schools are under a different order of authority. They stand very firmly *in loco parentis* and *in loco Deus*. Strangely enough this almost absolute investment of power creates in students not more hostility, but less. There are two reasons why this is so.

In the first place, the invidious idea that children are equals can make little headway, since the order of authority is so obviously hierarchical. In the second place the authority exercised is moral authority and not, as is increasingly the case with public schools, legal authority. Even where laws are made by consent of the governed, legal authority will always seem arbitrary unless it is perceived as corresponding with some natural or divine moral order. When it refers back only to majority will or only to itself (e.g., to previous legal decisions), it is on shaky ground. The civil rights movement was successful in changing hearts and minds to the extent that its leaders convinced other Americans that certain laws were out of line with the moral law.

The moral order has a more compelling hold on us than the legal order. The present Polish government has plenty of legal authority but little moral authority. It needs force because it cannot command loyalty. The reason is not difficult to see. It has miscalculated. Despite its impressive philosophical underpinnings, Communist ideology operates on the mistaken premise that the secular can get along without the sacred. Now this observation may seem a far cry from a discussion of American families, schools, and courts, but it is not so far. For all the differences that separate American society from Communist ones, we tend to act increasingly on the same premise. And we are not having much more luck with it than they.

THICK AND CLEAR RELIGIONS

The error in both cases lies in the belief that what C. S. Lewis called a "clear" religion is sufficient for enlisting the moral passions of a people. Lewis's distinction between "thick" and "clear" religions goes like this: thick religions are associated with smoky altars, sacrifice, deep mysteries, blood ties, mystical bonds, and communion with the gods. Clear religions, on the other hand, are demystified. They are tidy and rational, and claim to be based on principles of enlightenment and harmony. They promise illumination rather than salvation.[6] The Catholic Church is a prime example of the former, the Unitarian Church of the latter. Many modern philosophical and political theories, however, can be grouped into the second category since it is, in essence, a philosophical approach to belief. As Lewis saw it, the problem with a clear or "minimal" religion is that it has "no power to touch any of the deepest chords in our nature, or to evoke any response which will raise us even to a higher secular level." "A flag, a song, an old school tie is stronger than it," wrote Lewis.[7]

The same is true of rational, contractual societies and systems. Although they still require loyalty and fidelity, they are in no position to generate such things. This fact was not lost on our Founding Fathers. Robert Nisbet puts it this way:

> Just as Luther had solidly formed Roman Catholics in mind for the communicants of his antichurch Protestant sects, so the Founding Fathers and their counterparts in Europe had

---

[6] The contrast between the two types of religion is shown most strikingly in C. S. Lewis, *Till We Have Faces* (Grand Rapids: Eerdmans, 1966).

[7] C. S. Lewis, "Religion Without Dogma?" in Walter Hooper, ed., *God in the Dock* (Grand Rapids: Eerdmans, 1970), pp. 142, 143.

in their minds for democratic citizens men shaped by feudal-
ly grounded social and moral disciplines in family, community, and church.[8]

As a consequence, the Founders tried very hard to present
the new government as having a religious sanction ("laws of
nature and of nature's God . . . endowed by their Creator . . . our
sacred honor"). Lincoln, who also understood the poverty of the
naked state, was of a similar mind and felt no hesitation in giving
a bereaved mother the "thanks of the Republic" for having "laid
so costly a sacrifice upon the altar of freedom."[9]

But the reigning cultural orthodoxies are divorced from
that way of thinking. They are religions of the clear variety. Very
clear and thin, like water. They are presided over by people who,
to paraphrase Tom Bethell's description, think the world is in-
habited by people as devoid of passion as they are. They appeal
to intellectual types as does Unitarianism, but like Unitarianism
they instill little devotion in the ordinary man and woman. They
lack the requisite vision. Indeed, for the most part the present
culture seems to provide no more compelling a vision than television. The flags, songs, and "old school ties," the things that
make ordinary people feel bound to extraordinary responsibilities, are in short supply.

Above all, they fail to understand that blood really is
thicker than water. Certain roles such as those undertaken by
mothers and fathers require not just concern and enlightenment
but deep love, the kind of love that is given in full measure.
Bringing children into the world is literally a bloody sacrifice
and so, in some respects, is bringing them up. I am reminded of

---

[8] Robert Nisbet, *Prejudices* (Cambridge: Harvard University Press, 1982),
p. 127.
[9] Lincoln's letter to Mrs. Bixby quoted in Walter Berns, *For Capital
Punishment* (New York: Basic Books, 1979), p. 162.

a father who jokingly but proudly told me he had left half his skin on the walls of the playroom he had just built. It didn't speak much for his skill with hammer and saw, but it said a lot about his love for his children. There is not much in our current cultural ideology to suggest why he should love them that much. To explain it, you need to reach into that other category of deep and mysterious bonds which we now consider expendable. Families belong to the sacred order. Or call it the order of love.

We make a mistake to think we can deprive people of that old order of authority, and then expect them to have, for the new order, the kind of enthusiasm and loyalty which Odysseus felt for Ithaca. Our secular society still assumes those old bonds, even though it cannot produce them. It must stop polluting the wells from which they spring.

6

Storytelling and Virtue

I n *After Virtue* Alasdair MacIntyre observes that in all classical and heroic societies, "the chief means of moral education is the telling of stories."[1] In a real sense the heroes of
The Iliad and *The Odyssey* were the moral tutors of the Greeks.
Likewise, Aeneas was the model of heroic piety on which young
Romans were nurtured. Icelandic and Irish children were suck-
led on sagas. And the Christian world, which reaped the inheritance of both classical and heroic societies, carried on this tradition of moral education with Bible stories, stories from the lives
of saints, and stories of chivalry. To be educated properly was to
know of Achilles and Odysseus, Hector and Aeneas, and later to
know of Beowulf and Arthur and Percival and the Christian
story of salvation.

The telling of stories does not seem to hold a place of
much importance in contemporary attempts at moral education.
In most American and Canadian schools, the favored methods
for developing moral awareness are the moral reasoning approach of Harvard psychologist Lawrence Kohlberg and the
values clarification approach developed by University of Massachusetts psychologist Sidney Simon and his colleagues. These
models rely heavily on group discussion, analysis of competing
claims, and the development of decision-making skills. The closest approximation to a story is the presentation of a moral

---

[1] Alasdair MacIntyre, *After Virtue* (Notre Dame: University of Notre
Dame Press, 1981), p. 114.

dilemma: a man contemplates stealing a drug for his dying wife; passengers on a foundering lifeboat decide whether to toss their fellows overboard and who should be sacrificed; survivors in a fallout shelter debate whether to admit outsiders to their sanctuary.

It will be apparent at once that there are important differences between these modern "fables" and the old ones. And the differences give us, in turn, a clue to the differences in thinking that animate the modern as opposed to the classical and Christian approaches to moral education. The first difference is that no attempt is made to delineate character in the moral dilemma, whereas character is everything in the heroic story. In the saga or epic everything revolves around the character of the hero— whether he exercises or fails to exercise the virtues. But the characters in the dilemmas have no characters, only decisions to make. Both Heinz (the man in the purloined drug dilemma) and Ulysses must aid their wives, but there the comparison ends. Heinz is no Ulysses. He is a blank, a cipher. He is there because he is needed to present a dilemma. We have no interest in him, only in his case. One cannot imagine parents passing down to their children the saga of Heinz and the stolen drug.

The second difference is this: The actors in the dilemmas are not tied to any social particularities—traditions, loyalties, locations, or histories. True, Heinz is attached to his wife, but there is no indication why he should be. We know why Ulysses is loyal to Penelope, since her virtues are carefully enumerated. As in all the old stories, the hero's deeds are rooted in loyalty not only to homeland and tribe but also to hearth—essential details that are absent from the dilemmas.

It might be objected here that the modern dilemmas are intended not to tell stories but to embody principles or, more properly, the clash of principles: property rights, for example, versus the value of a human life, with the nod presumably going to the more universal value. But this is precisely the point I wish to make, for what is implied in this approach is that particular loves and loyalties—the kind that make for a good story—are largely irrelevant to moral issues. One can somehow dispense with the prelude of moral particularities and leap right into the arena of universal principles. The assumption is that the kernel of good moral judgment lies in abstract devotion to abstract principles. In Kohlberg's scheme, where justice is the sole guiding principle, one must leave mother and father, wife and husband, and cleave to the principle of Justice with capital *J.* Moreover, there is the suggestion that devotion to father and mother or attachment between wife and husband may have nothing to do with the pursuit of justice. As in so much contemporary psychology, the central concern is with the autonomous individual.

The third difference between the old stories and the new dilemmas is that the new stories, properly speaking, do not have endings. They are open-ended, unfinished. They await your judgment. What should the shelter survivors do next? You decide. Was Heinz right to steal the drug? You decide. There is, in short, no sense that the story is ever complete or definitive. It's up for grabs and will be again next year with the next class. You can do what you want with these stories; you cannot with *The Odyssey.* There is no sense of a life fully lived or a mission completed. All of which amounts to saying that they are not stories after all. The old storytelling approach to moral education has been replaced with something new.

The new approach is one from which the concepts of character and virtue are entirely missing. From its point of view, the life of a man is envisioned not as a personal story in which accumulated habits and actions may eventually harden into virtue or vice, but as a disconnected series of ethical and other dilemmas—all amenable to rational solution. If we return to the heroic, classical, and Christian stories, we can see how stark this contrast is and how radically novel the new approach is. And although the current techniques of moral education are largely the offspring of psychologists, we may note that the ancients had a more profound grasp of the psychology underlying moral education.

The telling of stories—as opposed to the presentation of open-ended dilemmas—implies first of all that adults have something to pass on to children, a valuable inheritance that children might not come by on their own. This is easy enough to accept about other cultures. "If we were anthropologists observing members of a tribe," writes Andrew Oldenquist, "it would be the most natural thing in the world to expect them to teach their morality and culture to their children and, moreover, to think that they had a perfect right to do so. . . ."[2] If we observed, he continues, that a society failed to do these things, we would conclude that they were "ruined, pitiable, alienated from their own values, and on the way out."[3] As I say, this is easy enough to see for other cultures, but when it comes to our own, a certain inhibition against cultural transmission sets in. A pervasive mentality of nondirectiveness and subjectiveness dictates that we don't have the right to impose our values on our children. And consequently we are forced to create the fiction that each child is in his own right a miniature Socrates—a moral philosopher, as Kohlberg would have it.

The traditional view is that adults do possess a moral treasure, and that to deprive children of it would in itself show a lack of virtue. We do not, to draw a rough analogy, wait until our children have reached the age of reason before suggesting that they brush their teeth. But sooner or later children will be able to figure out for themselves that brushing is a prudent practice. This is not necessarily true of moral practices. The

---

[2] Andrew Oldenquist, " 'Indoctrination' and Societal Suicide," *The Public Interest,* Spring 1981, p. 81.
[3] *Ibid.*

moral treasure can be acquired only in a certain way. And if it is not obtained in that way, it is not possessed at all. This is why Aristotle said that only those who have been well brought up can usefully study ethics. And why Plato maintained that the well-bred youth is nurtured from his earliest days to love the Good and the Beautiful "so that when Reason at length comes to him, then bred as he has been, he will hold out his hands in welcome and recognize her because of the affinity he bears to her."[4]

JUST SENTIMENTS

There is little chance that one who does not learn proper affections and just sentiments as a child will ever fully comprehend them. His knowledge, in short, will always be limited. What he can know will be determined by his sentiments, by dispositions and inclinations learned in childhood. A person who is not well habituated to virtue may come upon the fundamental principles of ethics, but he may never be able to grasp them properly. He comes upon them like an anthropologist stumbling upon tribal customs. He can describe them, write about them, analyze them, but he does not know them as an initiate knows them— even though the things he observes are his own cultural values. One cannot begin to understand the moral life until one begins to live it. Consequently, the autonomous moral explorer, because of his detached stance, is in no position to appreciate the practice of virtue, let alone practice it himself.

Writing on "the need for and inevitability of moral indoctrination," philosopher Bruce B. Suttle states: "If a person has no moral precepts and sensibilities, then those deficiencies cannot be corrected by offering the person moral reasons and evidence

---

[4]Plato, *Republic,* Book III.

for why he should acquire moral precepts and sensibilities. Without a general moral point of view, without a set of moral precepts and sensibilities, no moral arguments in support of having a moral point of view could be judged convincing, let alone recognized as moral arguments."[5]

What, then, is the proper form of education in regard to morality? It is, necessarily, an initiation, "men transmitting manhood to men," as C. S. Lewis puts it.[6] And this is best accomplished not by direct moral exhortation, but indirectly through example and practice. One cannot have classes in moral education. It is, rather, more like an apprentice learning from a master. "Lewis, like Aristotle," wrties Gilbert Meilander, "believes that moral principles are learned indirectly from others around us, who serve as exemplars. And he, again like Aristotle, suggests that it will be extremely difficult to develop virtuous individuals apart from a virtuous society."[7]

Yet, even in the most virtuous of societies adults, recognizing their own shortcomings, have seen the need to point to examples of moral wisdom and moral courage beyond themselves. Hence the reliance on heroic stories as the embodiment of cultural ideals. When virtues have fallen into desuetude, the need for stories about virtuous and courageous men, women, and children becomes more acute. Aware of this, Lewis created in *The Chronicles of Narnia* a literature of virtue of the type that can be considered both exemplar of and preparation for a mature morality. The *Narnia Chronicles* certainly seem to embody Aristotle's dictum that the aim of education is to make the pupil like and dislike what he ought.

------

[5] Bruce B. Suttle, "The Need for and Inevitability of Moral Indoctrination," *Educational Studies*, 12, No. 2 (Summer 1981), p. 156.

[6] C. S. Lewis, *The Abolition of Man* (New York: Macmillan, 1947), p. 33.

[7] Gilbert Meilander, *The Taste for the Other: The Social and Ethical Thought of C. S. Lewis* (Grand Rapids: Eerdmans, 1978), p. 212.

But if heroic stories provide examples we need to ask, examples of what? It would be a mistake to look upon the heroes of myth and epic as examples of autonomous moral agents or inventors of new moralities (as Nietzsche did), just as it would be a mistake to look upon them as stoic rule-abiders. The heroes of such stories are not moral philosophers, nor are they stoic. They are virtuous, or they strive to be virtuous. For classical and heroic societies and for those that sustain those traditions, morality is not a matter of following rules or making rules; it has to do with acquiring virtue. The virtues displayed by Achilles are what hold our attention, not any set of maxims he may expound. It is his loyalty to his friends that matters, not his loyalty to principle. Virtues are displayed in his actions, not only in what he says. The heroic man is not a moral pioneer who charts new ethics; rather, he is someone who does what ought to be done.

Even in the Gospel stories, the heroic theme is predominant. As I have written elsewhere, "There is nothing in Christ's attitude about himself to suggest that he saw himself mainly as a teacher. There is a strong suggestion that Jesus looked upon himself as someone who had a job to do. And the quality of that task was not unlike the quest of a Greek or Roman hero."[8] Christ does what is required. He comes to do the will of him by whom he was sent. He lays down his life for his friends, not for the sake of a principle.

Indeed, in the heroic literature there is usually very little question about what has to be done (most of the moral dilemmas in the Gospels are posed by the Pharisees); the question is whether the hero can resist temptation and do what he ought to do. Will his training in the virtues see him through?

---

[8] William K. Kilpatrick, *Psychological Seduction* (Nashville: Thomas Nelson, 1983), Chap. 9.

What is revealed in heroic stories is a profoundly realistic appraisal of behavior under conditions of combat—when it is dangerous to act as one ought or when a price will have to be paid. When the hero is weary, outnumbered, or alone, when his resources are depleted or temptation is overwhelming, he does better to rely on his acquired virtue than on his knack for moral philosophy. Likewise, most of us are thrown into situations where there is little time to weigh the moral pros and cons. Then the best question we can ask is, what do good men and women do in such situations? We are more likely to find an answer to that question if our training includes a thorough exposure to stories of virtue.

There are two other points to be noticed. First, the acquisition of virtue is never an individual project. Virtue is acquired through our own actions, but also through the actions of others. Virtue is always, in part, a gift. As MacIntyre notes, "There is no way to possess the virtues except as part of a tradition."[9] Acquiring virtue requires not the exercise of moral autonomy, but certain forms of submission. It requires the acceptance of standards set by others and even submission to forms of arduous training. The initiate to the virtuous life is the bearer of a tradition and owes respect to those who bore the tradition before he was born. Virtue, therefore, is rooted in particularities—the particularities of certain traditions, communities, and families. From that starting-point one can go on to a more universal morality, but as MacIntyre suggests, the notion of living completely in that universal realm is a dangerous illusion because such a step leads not to virtue, but to ideological obsession.

The second point is that training in virtue is an *education*

---

[9] *Op. cit.*, MacIntyre, *After Virtue*, p. 119.

sentimentale. MacIntyre defines virtues as "dispositions not only to act in particular ways but also to feel in particular ways."[10] The good man or woman is one who almost instinctively hates evil and loves what is right. This suggests why the telling of stories is a particularly good method of moral education, for it is widely recognized that stories have the power of eliciting sentiments that formal education does not. Stories alone are not sufficient, of course. Literary critic George Steiner reminds us that there is a type of literate person who responds to the cry in the book but turns a deaf ear to the cry in the streets.[11] Other forms of moral training are surely necessary. But since training in virtue is in part an *education sentimentale,* storytelling will be an important part of that training.

A logical corollary to this is that evenhanded, dispassionate discussions of values like those advocated by Kohlberg and Simon may undercut moral sentiments and impart the notion that moral questions are merely intellectual problems rather than human problems that naturally stir strong emotions. The very idea that all things are open to discussion and all values are to be accorded equal respect subtly undermines the virtuous instinct that some things are and ought to be repugnant and contemptible to the well-brought-up person. The nonjudgmental approach may thus tend to neutralize any character training that may have taken place. Once again, this may be good preparation for producing detached anthropologists, but it is a dubious form of moral education. Andrew Oldenquist states the matter well in observing that " 'Objective,' noncommittal discussions of our own moral principles, conducted as though one were discussing the mores of some distant tribe about which one

---

[10] *Ibid.,* p. 140.
[11] George Steiner, *Language and Silence* (New York: Atheneum, 1967), p. 5.

cares nothing, will lead young people to sense that it is not *morality* that is being discussed, and, perhaps, to view their own moral community as though it were that distant tribe."[12]

THRESHOLD OF TOLERANCE

If virtue is a matter of habituation, so is vice. In fact, the kind of morally neutral discussion of values mentioned above can easily become a form of desensitization to thinking in terms of either virtue or vice. One gets habituated instead to thinking in terms of rights, wants, and needs. This nonjudgmental atmosphere, which is not confined to the moral education classroom but rather has become all-pervasive, prepares the way for more blatant forms of desensitization. Enter the media with their penchant for discussing any and all topics with the neutral attitude of the talk show host. Enter the advertiser who steadily advances into areas that were once thought too private or too important to be exploited. Enter the sociologists and the psychologists with explanations and excuses for criminal behavior. Enter the gratuitous depiction of violence on the screen. Enter pornography. One becomes used to it all. One's threshold of tolerance is raised higher and higher. Moral sensitivities acquired in childhood—if they ever were acquired—begin to erode.

"Blush, blush, thou lump of foul deformity," cries Lady Anne to Richard III. But like Shakespeare's Richard, many of us have long since lost the capacity to blush. Where habits of virtue do not prosper, it is certain that habituation to vice will. It is important to note that we are talking here primarily about habitual responses, not necessarily about habitual actions. The fact that individuals can continue to refrain from vicious deeds does not prevent a gradual erosion of proper moral sentiments. And

---

[12] *Op. cit.*, Oldenquist, " 'Indoctrination'. . . ," p. 90.

the erosion of these sentiments in those who still maintain a moral life contributes to the climate that permits the pornographer, the drug pusher, and the rapist to flourish.

Habituation is a fact of life as surely in our time as it was in Aristotle's. The difference perhaps is that only the advertisers, the media, and the promoters still recognize that fact. This gives them an enormous advantage over the naive majority, who cling piously to the belief that values are somehow self-created when, in fact, their values are the playthings of the desensitizers. For desensitization is the engine of the current moral upheaval. Thirty years ago C. S. Lewis contemplated the possibility of an "abolition of man"—an alteration of human nature that would remove man's moral nature.[13] The first step would be a deconditioning process, "the stifling of all deep-set repugnancies."[14]

Perhaps the most disconcerting aspect of this kind of desensitization is that the more effectively it is carried out, the less likely are its victims to have any awareness of what is happening. Those who have been well conditioned are usually the last to know. Such an analysis suggests that whatever lack of sophistication they may suffer from, the Moral Majority have a keener eye for the current moral climate than the representatives of Kohlberg's school of thought.

A VISION OF LIFE

What, to return to the central theme of this chapter, do stories have to do with all this? Just this: Stories of virtue, courage, and justice can and should play a central part in the formation of good habit—that is, in the formation of character. Stories pro-

---

[13] *Op. cit.*, Lewis, *The Abolition of Man.*
[14] C. S. Lewis, *That Hideous Strength* (New York: Macmillan, 1946), p. 203.

91

vide a way of habituating children to virtue. They help to instill proper sentiments. They reinforce indirectly the more explicit moral teaching of family, church, and school. They provide also a defense against the relentless process of desensitization that goes on in modern societies. And they provide a standard against which erosion of standards can be measured.

In addition, stories expand the imagination. Moral development is not simply a matter of becoming more rational or acquiring decision-making skills. It has to do with vision, the way one looks at life. Indeed, moral evil and sin are sometimes described by theologians as an inability to see rightly. Conversely, moral improvement is often described (by very ordinary people as well as theologians) as the result of seeing things in a different light or seeing them for the first time. "I was blind, but now I see" is more than a line from an old hymn; it is the way a great many people look at their moral growth. It is therefore entirely inadequate to explain morality in terms of developmental stages, as Kohlberg does. The tranformation of the moral life is rarely effected without a transformation of imagination. It follows that one of the central tasks of moral education is to nourish the imagination with rich and powerful images of the kind found in stories, myths, poems, biography, and drama. If we wish our children to grow up with a deep and adequate vision of life, we must provide a rich fund for them to draw on.[15]

What's more, stories appeal to the child's normal need for identification, which is a need not for finding others just like himself (the mistake of so much contemporary children's literature), but for finding others who are better than himself—who are just like he might become if he fulfills his potential for

---

[15] For a fuller discussion of "visional" ethics, see Stanley Hauerwas, *Vision and Virtue* (Notre Dame: University of Notre Dame Press, 1981), and Craig Dykstra, *Vision and Character* (New York: Paulist Press, 1981).

goodness. Identification, therefore, is built on pretense, but there is such a thing as good pretense. C. S. Lewis, in writing about his own development, admits to a certain hypocrisy when in the company of an army friend, a man of deep conscience. He then says, "The distinction between pretending you are better than you are and beginning to be better in reality is finer than moral sleuthhounds conceive."[16]

PURE HEARTS AND KINDLY KINGS

Not just any stories will do, however. Though realistic stories about boys and girls just like oneself probably do no harm, they fail to enlarge the imagination in the way that heroic stories do. But we must also be clear about what we mean by a hero. Heroic stories link strength or cunning or resourcefulness with virtue. Galahad's strength is as the strength of ten because his heart is pure. Beowulf, who has the strength of thirty men in his grip, is also renowned as "the kindest of worldly kings." The cunning of Ulysses is used in the service of loyalty to his men. In the old epics the superheroes' qualities do not end with raw power. But that seems to be a current trend. Consider the popularity of "The Hulk"—a former television series spun off the comic book of the same name. The Hulk, hardly human, is more like a force of nature; he appears to be, for the most part, amoral.

Moral literature need not be of epic proportions. There is also a place for stories of manners and duty, decency and virtue, loyalty and friendship on a less epic scale—stories that say, in effect, however ordinary people actually behave toward one another, this is how they ought to behave. *The Little House on*

---

[16] C. S. Lewis, *Surprised by Joy* (New York: Harcourt, Brace & World, 1955), pp. 192, 193.

the Prairie, The Wind in the Willows, and *The Hobbit* (a combination of heroism and hominess) come to mind as examples of this type of literature. Younger children need stories that are similar but much shorter and can be told orally.

It might be a mistake to inundate a child with too many stories. But it is important that the right kind of stories be repeated over and over until they are nearly learned by heart. After all, if repetition were not such an effective technique in the education of habits, we can be certain that the advertisers would long since have ceased to employ it.

7

Youth's Frontier: Making Ethical Decisions

An Evaluation*

---

* *Youth's Frontier* is the title of a new Boy Scout manual on making ethical decisions.

The Boy Scouts' new ethical decision-making guide is, on balance, a good thing. It's not uniformly good—there are occasional vacillations and occasional lapses into jargon—but the good outweighs the bad. Fortunately, it's not too difficult to separate the good from the bad. The good parts are those in which the authors talk like Boy Scout leaders, and the bad parts are those in which they talk like psychologists. The weaknesses that exist come from the attempt to blend the Boy Scout philosophy with some recent psychological programs of moral education—specifically, the values clarification approach and the moral reasoning approach.

The attempted blending doesn't work because, like oil and water, these two philosophies don't mix. The Scout Oath and Scout Law are anchored in a tradition (a very ancient tradition) called "character ethics." In this tradition, ethical behavior is a factor of the kind of person you are, and consequently much stress is put on habit formation and the acquisition of the virtues. The psychological models of moral education, on the other hand, belong to a more recent philosophic tradition which goes under many names but has most usefully been characterized as "quandary ethics." Quandary ethics concerns itself mainly with problem solving. Moral problems, on this view, are not unlike problems in business or social policy. To solve problems, one needs to be well informed, employ rational strategies, weigh the alternatives, etc. Proponents of this school would tend to view a badly behaved youth not as someone who lacks character, but as someone who lacks decision-making skills. Various classroom exercises, consisting mainly of ethical dilemmas, are designed to help students acquire such skills.

The title of the Scout document—*Making Ethical Decisions*—is, of course, a bow to this second school of thought. But it is an ill-considered concession to what is, essentially, the opposition. Quandary ethicists, particularly of the psychological wing of quandary ethics, have no use for character or character development. They are not interested in virtue or how it is acquired. For example, Lawrence Kohlberg (developer of the moral reasoning approach) has repeatedly rejected what he calls "the bag of virtues" approach to inculcating morality.

But what else is the Scout Law except a "bag of virtues"? And how many organizations are as explicitly in the business of building character as are the Scouts? If building character is what the Scouts are about, they will want to carefully assess the utility of decision-making and classroom discussion models. While the weighing and calculating and cool-neutrality characteristic of the quandary approach may be appropriate for preparing statesmen to ponder world issues, there is much to suggest that it is all wrong for purposes of building character. And much to suggest that it may (as many of its critics claim) actually undermine whatever character formation has gone on in the home.

Most societies have recognized that in matters of individual morality, it is the stock response, not the carefully cultivated one, that counts. This comes down to a simple sense of duty or of loyalty, of doing what is required of any decent person in the same situation. The stock response develops in a climate where certain values are assumed and not questioned, and where age mates and their leaders are bound together by common projects, common adventures, common rituals, and common allegiance to some higher authority. Another important way we learn stock responses is through example, and this would include examples from stories and legends and everyday life—the type of story where ordinary boys and girls, men and women, give up their free time to help others, tell the truth at great personal cost, survive hardship through prayer and courage, and, yes, even pull victims from icy ponds.

Stock responses may, of course, be dismissed as conditioned or unreflective, but most people realize they go much deeper than that. They are appealing to us in the first place because they seem to refer back to something fundamental—God's law, or the natural law, or simple goodness.

The point is that stock responses can be dissolved (or may never take hold in the first place) in the climate of subjectivism, decision-making, and weighing of alternatives recommended by the quandary ethicist. And that is too bad, because although stock responses may not be the thing we need for negotiating the Mideast crisis, they are the thing that prevents everyday life from degenerating into exploitation and savagery.

For some reason the authors of this new Boy Scout program feel compelled to pay lip service to the new psychology. Fortunately, however, they have a more solid allegiance to the Scout mission, and consequently they do not hesitate to do what most people who advertise themselves as moral educators would never do—that is, they have the courage to make distinctions between right and wrong, and to recommend honesty, obedience, courage, loyalty, service, forgiveness, and the "guidance of God's commandments." And when they do offer ethical dilemmas, they have the audacity to tell the reader what the right decision is. Bravo!

Still, it would be wise for the Scouts not to overestimate the value of such formal programs. There are much more effective methods of moral formation than the "let's sit down and talk about morality" approach. They have to do with attitudes and actions and rituals that already assume a moral core. In groups that are sure and confident of their role and proud of their rituals and beliefs, much of that moral foundation can be left unspoken. It is only when groups become unconfident and self-doubting that they begin to offer courses in morality.

The Boy Scouts might take as a cautionary tale an interesting study in which the effects of Outward Bound programs
on delinquents were compared with the effects of reform
school. The delinquents who went through the Outward Bound
programs were found to have a much lower return-to-crime
rate. The study ought to be heartening to Scout leaders because,
of course, many Scout activities parallel Outward Bound activities, and apparently such activities and such organizations can
have a real transformative power. The cautionary part of the
story is this: despite the overall results, one of the Outward
Bound groups actually did no better with its delinquents than
did the reform schools—and that was the group that decided to
add on to its usual activities an intensive program of sensitivity
groups. Although the parallel between that situation and the
current situation of the Scouts is only a very rough one, it still
ought to raise questions about the general utility of talk sessions
in promoting moral behavior.

8

"They're Going to Do It Anyway"

One of the arguments I hear most frequently when morally permissive measures are challenged is the formula, "they're going to do it anyway." For example, it seems to be the main argument in opposition to the "squeal rule" (the seemingly ill-fated proposal which would require parents to be notified when their minor children seek contraceptives). Teenagers are going to have sex anyway, runs the argument, and we just increase the risk for them when we make it difficult to obtain information about birth control. A similar argument is advanced in favor of doing nothing about the increased sexual suggestiveness of television and the open display of sex magazines in drugstores or convenience stores: "Kids are going to find out about those things anyway."

But is it really true that "they'll do it anyway"? Some young people will, of course, go ahead and do what they want to do regardless. The question, however, is not what some will do, but what most will do. No social policy can ever be expected to bring all citizens into line; we only hope that it will have that effect on most. In some ways the issue is similar to that concerning the deterrent effect of punishment on crime. It is sometimes argued that those who commit crimes are going to do so anyway; consequently severity of punishment won't stop them. When we consider actual criminals, this argument seems quite strong. After all, whatever deterrence there was, was not enough. But the question is not, "What would it take to prevent this convicted thief or that convicted embezzler from committing a crime?" but rather, "What would it take to prevent me?" As Ernest Van den Haag points out in *Punishing Criminals,*

"Not all can be restrained by the prohibition and by the threat of punishment, however severe. But most can be." The true test of the deterrent effect, then, would be to remove the penalties for crimes and observe what happens next. Would crimes continue to be committed only by what we call the criminal class? Or would we see a large increase in the membership of the criminal class? How many of us, to use Van den Haag's illustration, would continue in the habit of buying train tickets if it became known that there are no conductors on the trains anymore?

Immoral behavior is no more immune to penalties than criminal behavior. If, to return to the "squeal rule," we make it difficult for teenagers to obtain birth control information or assistance, it does not follow that they will all go ahead with their plans anyway. Some will. Perhaps many will not. If the level of risk, inconvenience, and stigma is sufficiently high, most of us learn to govern or control our instincts. Of course, nothing will make a difference unless there are some prior internal restraints. External threats and sanctions by themselves are not enough to make us toe the line; but threats, sanctions, and stigmas do help reinforce and strengthen internal restraints. Perhaps if adults did make it more difficult for teenagers to engage in sexual activity, some young people would have the excuse they needed to resist pressure and temptation.

It may well be, then, that the reason "They're going to do it anyway" has less to do with irresistible human instincts, and more to do with the fact that society has adopted the attitude, "They're going to do it anyway." Why weren't "they" doing "it" anyway in the thirties and forties and fifties? The incidence of delinquency, crime, and teenage pregnancy was considerably lower than it is today. In the Great Depression, when people had more excuse to bend the rules, the rate of crime actually dropped. A large part of the reason for this difference is simply that people then had different expectations about what people would and should do. And those expectations were widely known and reinforced on all social levels.

Whenever this attitude of "They're going to do it anyway" is adopted, the "it" in the equation is revealed to have an insatiable appetite for expansion, so that the "it" "they" were doing yesterday seems almost innocent in comparison with the "it" "they" are doing today and the "it" "they" will demand to do tomorrow. The attitude is in reality an invitation to push the boundaries of decency further and further back. Those who adopt this myth always end up capitulating to whatever it is people happen to be doing today. And they insure that more of it will happen in the future. As Joseph Sobran points out, "Abortion 'happened anyway' before it was legalized. It happens much more commonly now."

In some senses the myth of "They're going to do it anyway" is similar to the myth which says, "You can't legislate morality." As a matter of fact, however, we can and do legislate morality. Edmond Cahn demonstrates this point in *The Moral Decision* by citing an incident in Fielding's *Joseph Andrews*. Joseph has been set upon by thieves, beaten, and stripped of his clothing. A stagecoach comes by, but none of the passengers are moved by compassion. The coachman wants his fare, the old gentleman fears assault, the lady is offended by his nakedness. However, an equally unsympathetic passenger who happens to be a lawyer reminds them that if Joseph dies they might be called to account under the law. And this legislative fact slowly works to change their attitude toward Joseph, and even leads one passenger to genuine compassion.

I think there can be little doubt that civil rights legislation in this country has had the same effect. Laws granting equality of access to blacks in the South may have been hated and grudgingly obeyed at first. Nevertheless, in obeying the law over a long period of time certain habits are induced which eventually alter attitudes and even bring about a change of heart. The law has an educative function as well as a judicial one, and if it can work to change hearts entrenched in racial bitterness, there is no reason it cannot also work to change sexual habits as well.

A "squeal" law by itself will not do the trick, of course, but it should not be cast aside on the unwarranted assumption that human instincts are uncontrollable. We are cultural as well as instinctual creatures, and as a consequence public policy does shape private morality.

9

A Book Review by William Kirk Kilpatrick

WHEN BAD THINGS HAPPEN TO GOOD PEOPLE
By Harold S. Kushner (New York: Schocken, 1981)

This is the kind of book that is called "honest" and "courageous" by the literary establishment. When these accolades descend on a book about religion, it is a good bet that the author is going to tell us we have to grow up, stop thinking of God as a Heavenly Parent, and find within ourselves "the courage to become" or some equivalent capacity.

This best seller by Rabbi Harold Kushner of Temple Israel in Natick, Massachusetts is very much in that vein. Since Kushner cannot believe in a God who allows suffering, he replaces him with a God of his own invention, who is angered and saddened at suffering but cannot do anything to stop it. God, like us, is in a process of becoming. He can only do so much. The rest is up to us.

The real question, then, is not "Who is to blame for tragedy?" but "Now that this has happened, what shall I do about it?" Another way of stating the problem is to ask, "What do we do with our pain so that it becomes meaningful?" This, of course, is a good question. Pain that has meaning is more endurable than pain that seems pointless. Kushner's answer, however, is not satisfying. The bad things that happen to us do not have any meaning, he says, but "we can give them a meaning." We can redeem senseless tragedies by "imposing meaning on them."

Rabbi Kushner is hard on those whose views on suffering differ from his, so let me be hard on him. The use of the word "imposing" betrays an attitude toward suffering that may in some senses be considered elitist. In many respects this is a book for the successful—for those who either have made or can make a success out of their tragedy, who have the strength or courage (or opportunities) to pull themselves together again "by choosing to go on living and creating new life," and by reaching out to others. This is quite different from the idea of "finding" a meaning in suffering (as, for example, in Victor Frankl's book *Man's Search for Meaning,* or in the Christian view). The latter view allows for the possibility of finding meaning in continued passive suffering and therefore offers hope to people whose circumstances or abilities simply will not allow them to triumph over adversity. Kushner's view seems to leave such people out in the cold. In reading his book, one gets the impression that suffering can be considered meaningful only if some tangible earthly good comes out of it.

By taking such a tack, the author inadvertently sets the stage for "blaming the victim"—an attitude he himself criticizes in the early part of the book. God cannot prevent pain, says Kushner, but afterwards he gives us the strength and courage to start again. If that is so, and if God distributes his aid equally as Kushner implies, then some people can be blamed for not doing as much with this help as others, since it is clear that some bear tragedy less ably than others. Kushner doesn't say this in so many words, but it is the logical conclusion of his position.

The underlying problem with Kushner's analysis is that, despite his backhanded defense of God, he writes from within a time-bound framework. This life is all we know. The good for man begins and ends with this world. Anything else is "wishful thinking." If that is so, then it sems to me that others (such as Schopenhauer) have looked at suffering in a more courageous and unblinking fashion. "The dead," writes Kushner, "depend on us for their redemption and immortality." Yet, by "immortality" he clearly means living on in memory. And how long do any but the very famous live on in memory? And what will become of their memory when the whole race is gone, as someday it must?

A really honest view compels us to admit that if there is no ultimate meaning, there is no meaning at all. If this life is the whole show, it will not matter in the long run whether you die accidentally at eighteen or peacefully at eighty. And all this business about creating or imposing meaning is whistling in the dark.

10
The Pope's Dream

The other day I read an article in *The New York Review of Books* about the German theologian Karl Rahner. The article recounts a dream of Rahner's in which the Pope meets with the leading representatives of the other Christian churches to discuss the question of his own infallibility. In Rahner's hopeful dream, "a very congenial Pontiff calls the others 'gentlemen, dear brothers' and promises, for the sake of unification of the churches, to be extremely circumspect in any future exercise of infallibility and one even gets the impression that he might not invoke it anymore." The others "are on the brink of uniting with Rome when Rahner wakes up."

It so happens that I also had a dream about the Pope, and reading this article brought it to mind. My dream, like Rahner's, concerns infallibility, and by a coincidence my Pontiff is also a congenial fellow. The exact identity of the Pope is unclear, although a good guess can be made. The truth is that in my dream, I seem to be the Pope. In dreams, of course, personal identity tends to be ambiguous and doesn't seem that crucial anyway except to psychiatrists. And besides, with the Pope it's the office that counts, not the man; so I will henceforth refer to my dream Pope in the third person.

In my dream it seems that the Pope no longer lives in the Vatican palace, but in a medium-size house with a red tile roof in a suburb of Rome, a pleasant suburb which might easily be mistaken for an American suburb. The only thing which distinguishes the Pope's house from those of his neighbors is that he happens to have a small tool shed in the back yard. To make ends meet, the Pope rents out three rooms in his house. Popes are now expected to help support themselves, what with the more austere economic climate. Over and above the general hard times must be added the fact that several years before, the Church, in an expression of human solidarity, had divested itself of much of its wealth, including the Vatican living quarters (which were now remodeled as condominiums) and Castel Gandolfo, which had, after all, been terribly expensive to heat and maintain. The jewels and gold and gemmed tiaras had also gone. The money from the sale of these various assets had gone to several worthy programs for the alleviation of world hunger. The rest of the world had been much impressed by these actions, although a few ideological extremists charged that it was only a propaganda ploy, and some Third World leaders hinted broadly that it was only a handout, and that, in fact, the Church was holding back.

But the reality of the situation is that the Church is making do on a modest budget. So, despite the honor that still accrues to the Pope, he is expected to pull his own weight. Well, the Pope is doing that. His rental income takes care of his personal needs and helps considerably with the mortgage payments. The Pope rents out to young respectable working people who are afforded kitchen privileges. In truth, they pretty much have the run of the house. Happily for all, it's a compatible mix. They like the Pope and each other, and he likes them. His household provides a comfortable retreat from the tensions of his job and the formalities of holding an important office.

There is a problem, however, an awkward situation.

It seems that the Pope has a nephew who is slightly retarded. In addition, the boy (he's eighteen) is a behavior problem. He's not quite a delinquent, but he has, as the social workers say, "poor impulse control." Very poor impulse control. There are psychiatric problems as well, but there is no need to go into them here. The important thing is that the boy's family can no longer cope with him, and won't. He's been through foster homes also, and that hasn't worked. Right now he's out on the streets, somehow making do; but it's obvious that he will shortly end up in some sort of institution. This boy is not a particularly likable boy, either. He hasn't been trained well, and his personal habits of dress and cleanliness leave much to be desired. To be perfectly honest, the Pope doesn't have much fondness for the boy, but then neither does anyone else. As we have seen, his parents have washed their hands of him. In their defense, it should be mentioned that they have problems of their own: marital troubles and other children to raise.

This problem is really not the Pope's responsibility. Everybody recognizes that. After all, as Pope he has other, overriding responsibilities: the care of the entire flock, world peace, and so on. In addition, he's never been close with that branch of the family, and besides there are plenty of other family members who have an equal if not greater responsibility than the Pope. It's not as though the Pope has a great many resources at hand either; he is only just getting by himself, and his other brothers and sisters are doing quite well in comparison. But no one else seems willing to take responsibility for the boy. They have written him off and perhaps justifiably so. After all, some people are just never going to make it no matter how much you do for them.

The Pope, however, has a strong sense of duty. A Christian, particularly a Christian pastor, he feels, ought to be the servant of all. Indeed, the Pope's humility and sense of duty were doubtless the key factors in his election. He knew well enough that his elevation certainly had nothing to do with his scholarship or political savvy. But he was a good pastor, and when, because of a deadlock in the voting, it was found necessary to choose a compromise candidate, they turned to him. He reminded people of John XXIII.

One solution the Pope toyed with was to ask one of his roomers to leave. The thought of this made him gloomy. Not only did he hate to part with any of his roomers—his friends really—but he would now have to share his life with a difficult and disagreeable young man. On top of this, he would lose one third of his income since the nephew was clearly in no position to pay for the room. If that happened, the Pope was not at all certain he would be able to maintain his payments to the bank. In the back of his mind lurked the dark possibility that he might even lose his home. He had grown quite fond of it, as proud homeowners will.

Yes, the Pope was quite gloomy. So were his neighbors. In a small suburban community, news of this type gets around. The townsfolk knew of the Pope's plight and were sympathetic—not so sympathetic, of course, that any of them were about to take the boy into their own households. Who could blame them? Still, they were good people, and they suffered with him.

For weeks, the Pope put off any decision about what he should do. He hoped that somehow, something would happen to relieve him of this responsibility. But, of course, nothing did happen.

It was then that the Pope discovered the addition to his house. Late one night the Pope found himelf unable to sleep— although perhaps he was dreaming, and only dreamed he was unable to sleep. Indeed, at this point in my dream it is entirely possible that the Pope himself is dreaming. Who can tell for sure? It's hard to say exactly what transpires in a dream. This is because of its dreamlike quality. In any event, in his dream or in his sleepless condition, the Pope finds himself wandering into the kitchen for a snack. It's a nice, neat modern kitchen, well lighted, with ceramic tile behind the counters. The outer wall features a large picture window looking out on the back yard.

Perhaps the Pope had never paid much attention before; he has been busy, and he hasn't lived here that long. But now, looking out the window he notices something he had not noticed before. Something quite incredible, really. It is an extension to his house—neat and compact with a red tile roof just like the main house. The Pope can hardly believe his eyes, but there it is. It is amazing that he has never noticed it before. Now, the Pope is a levelheaded man and not given to wish-fulfillment fantasies. The thought immediately comes into his head that this is only a dream and, as will often happen in dreams, one sometimes discovers a new room or two in one's house.

But if this is a dream, it is a very clever mimic of reality because, after all, the Pope does really seem to be awake. And now he notices a door leading off the kitchen in the direction of the extension. Try as he might, the Pope can't suppress a great sense of expectancy and the beginnings of a vast feeling of relief. Premature perhaps, because, of course, he is still not sure. But his skepticism is dying fast. A short hallway off the kitchen door leads him to another door and then into the kitchen of the addition. Yes, it has a kitchen of its own—or a kitchenette, to be accurate, and there is a small bedroom and a bath and a sitting room. It is what Americans call a mother-in-law apartment.

The Pope has learned not to expect much from life; this is far more than he had ever expected. It is nothing less than the solution to the problem. This is the perfect place for his nephew to live—or is it his aged and infirm mother? In my dream it seems to be first one, then the other. At any rate, the situation seems now to be far more hopeful. The boy can have a place to stay, but he won't be in the main house. There will be less chance of the other roomers becoming alienated, less chance that the Pope's comfortable present arrangement will be threatened. The Pope now remembers that a community social agency has promised to send a worker to visit the boy three times a week and teach him housekeeping skills. This will limit the Pope's own responsibility. Not that he wouldn't welcome his nephew into the main house at any time. Still, it wouldn't be all the time. Some distance could be maintained. Yes, things are looking up. Given the new situation, there is reason to hope that all will work out well.

The Pope is elated, and the next day he loses no time in showing his discovery to his housemates. They are equally amazed and pleased, as is the entire neighborhood once the word gets around. It is indeed a handsome addition to the house, and it is a wonder no one had noticed it before. Apparently you just have to look at it in the right way. All of this comes as a secret relief to the Pope, who up to this point had still harbored a fear that it was only a dream.

"That's quite a dream house you've got for yourself now," says his neighbor Barzini, nudging him in a friendly way.

The Pope smiles shyly and shrugs. "C'mon up and I'll show you around."

Soon enough the wire services pick up the story, and something like a general sigh of relief goes up all over the Christian world because by this point the Pope's problem had become a general concern. People hated to see this good man, who had so many cares, have to wrestle with this extra dilemma. More than that, people so closely identified with the good-hearted Pope that his personal problems seemed to be theirs also. And a solution to this problem seemed nothing less than a solution to a great problem the whole Church had long grappled with.

The solution seemed so simple and yet so decisive that in many minds it began to take on the stature of a major break-through—a new departure for the Church, and one that had long been needed. In some way that was not quite clear but deeply felt, the new addition was seen as representing the answer to many questions that had plagued the Church.

It was no surprise, then, that before long key people in the community and in the Church were thinking of ways to secure this new understanding of the Pope's house. Soon enough, what with one thing leading to another, people were openly suggesting that what was needed was an infallible proclamation. Such a thing had not been done for decades, but opinion was quickly building that if anything was important enough to have the seal of infallibility set on it, it was this. This idea grasped people's imaginations so thoroughly and so powerfully that it hardly seemed necessary to think about. It seemed inevitable, something that had to happen—an incoming tide, champagne spouting from an uncorked bottle.

The Pope received these overtures with welcome. He was as anxious as anyone else to have the matter finally resolved. And, moreover, resolved quickly; for the Pope now felt a certain sense of urgency, a premonition that a delay might somehow be fatal to this new hope. Something about the whole situation bothered him, though he couldn't quite say what.

He had, besides, many other pastoral concerns that needed his attention. Just today, for instance, he was giving an audience to representatives of the International Brotherhood of Catholic Thieves. Earlier in the week it had been the Catholic Democratic Union of Murderers and Rapists. The argument was familiar to the Pope. The spokesman for the thieves, a wiry Italian fellow with a large mustache and expressive eyes, was making the case that the commandment against stealing put an intolerable burden on his people.

"Holy Father, I implore you," he was saying, "all we ask is the right to determine our own conscience. Aren't we all equal as God's children? Why must we be made to feel like second-class citizens of the Church? Doesn't every man have a right to pursue his profession with dignity and honor . . ."

(Here he quoted from a papal encyclical.)

He finally concluded, "Holy Father, let us reason together. Let us find a way to remove this burden of guilty feelings."

The Holy Father was moved by this appeal, though he was disturbed by the phrase "guilty feelings." That seemed not quite right. He was not sure either whether he should address these people as "my brothers in Christ," but he always did, even last month's delegation from the American Society of Catholic Transsexuals. The Pope assured the thieves that he would give the matter prayerful consideration. That made one more difficult decision to add to a growing list, for the pontiff had been deferring all of these painful choices in the vague hope that the passage of time would either resolve them or make them go away.

Somehow all these things were bound up in his mind with the pending proclamation on the addition to his house. That was the key: the symbolic act which would signal an easing of consciences all around. The Pope had already decided on a title for it—*Mansiones Multae,* Many Mansions.

That would be the key. The whole idea of keys, however, disturbed the Holy Father. These days whenever he went on his Vatican rounds, his eyes would focus on the heavy crossed keys in the papal coat of arms. (Most of the symbolic heraldry had been retained as a sop to Church conservatives.) They did not look like the keys to a mother-in-law apartment.

The more the Pope thought about the matter, the more bothered he became. Even the continual assurances of his staff did not help—in fact, only seemed to make matters worse. They were of one mind that the proclamation was a move in the right direction, and they were the experts: canon lawyers, theologians, and bishops, of course, but also psychologists and social work professionals. Actually, the latter two groups were in the majority. But the preponderance of social workers and psychologists on the Vatican staff did not seem strange to the Pope or to anyone else. It had been a gradual accretion, and one that seemed in line with the Church's concern for the person.

In any event it was not this pressure—if pressure it could be called—that weighed most heavily with the Pope. Rather it was the opinion of his friends and neighbors that most concerned him. The discovery of the added apartment had taken on a great significance for them. They were pleased for the Pope, and they were pleased for themselves that they were the Pope's neighbors. Indeed, they were so proud that they had somehow managed to arrange for the *ex cathedra* pronouncement to be made in the public square of their own suburban village. He did not want to disappoint them.

But a certain thought had now insinuated itself into his head. It was all very well, he thought, for his friends and neighbors to be excited over the coming pronouncement; they could afford to be happy because, when all was said and done, it wasn't their responsibility. He had, in addition, the uncomfortable thought that a man who sat in the papal throne and spoke *ex cathedra* was obligated by other bonds than friendship.

Now it is the eve of the pronouncement. The Pope tosses and turns these thoughts in his mind like a man tossing and turning at the end of a long and disturbing dream. It is still dark, but the Pope senses that morning is near. He wishes he had more time. Everything seems to have happened too swiftly. Grave doubts assail him. Is there really an addition to his home? The more he thinks about it, the more he fears it has been only a dream. The unconscious loves to play tricks on the tired mind. One second he is sure it is there and the next . . . He had better check again. Once more the Pope goes down to the kitchen and over to the window, although he now senses that he may be only dreaming he is doing this. Once, he remembers, he had dreamed he had gotten up, shaved, and dressed, and then woke up to find he was still in bed.

The window reveals what the Pope already knows. There is nothing to be seen except the back lawn and the tool shed. Of course there is nothing! He realizes immediately that there has never been an addition.

"Damn these dreams," he mutters, but to tell the truth his disappointment at finding his house reduced is mingled with relief. Both feelings soon give way, however, to acute embarrassment, for he knows what he must do.

The next day is the day of the pronouncement. For some reason the Pope finds himself that morning in shirt sleeves mingling with a group of neighbors on the street outside his house. They are exchanging comments about how nice the addition looks and how well it fits into the neighborhood. The Pope can see clearly now that his house is as it has always been: a modest red-tiled villa with a matching tool shed in the back—but no extension. But he understands that it is no use trying to correct them—not just yet. He would only be wasting his energy standing here in his shirt sleeves arguing. And he needs his energy.

Later in the afternoon the Pontiff, dressed in plain cloth vestments and a plain tiara, is led in solemn procession to the throne now installed on a raised dais in the sunlit square. Happy faces greet him as he makes his way slowly forward. People take care, though, not to shout or clap. They know how to act when a solemn observance is being solemnly observed. The Pope, however, is sad. The nearer he approaches to the throne, the sadder he becomes. He understands quite plainly now, and the realization that he is the one to whom this understanding has been entrusted weighs him nearly to the ground. Sometimes in a dream you will try to walk or run and find that you can hardly move your legs. It is that way for the Pope now. His feet seem to be cast in bronze; and it is only with great effort that he mounts the steps to the dais.

As the Pontiff sits down, the murmur of expectancy which surrounds him dies into a hushed silence. The doctrine of the Pope's house is about to become infallible. A rolled parchment is placed into his hand: the revision he had prepared only that morning. The Pope had insisted on sealing it himself. Now he breaks open the seal—the bulla—and unrolls the parchment.

"*Domus aedificata super petram . . .*" he intones in cadenced Latin: "A house built upon a rock will withstand many storms. But a house founded on wishes is no better than a house of cards. The Church, which is entrusted with the care and shelter of souls, may not gamble in such a careless fashion. . . ."

This is not exactly what the Pope had written that morning. The part about "house of cards" and "gambling" had not been in the original, but it was the gist of what he wanted to say, and now the words seemed to flow from his lips with a power of their own.

". . . And so, my dear brothers and sisters, it is with

heartfelt sadnsss and humility that we must proclaim to you that there is no addition to the Pope's house. And we must condemn as error the false understanding of our house which, unfortunately, we ourselves have helped to foster. . . ."

The Pope went on to say many more things, not only about speculative additions, but also about simple everyday concerns such as murder, theft, and lying. Exactly what he did say, however, I cannot tell you. I had already been half awake when the Pope began his talk, and then my dream faded completely. I toyed with the idea of attempting to go back to sleep and finish it, but I know that doesn't often work. And, besides, I wanted to check something in the kitchen.

11

Encounters with the Quiet Revolutionary

One of America's most revolutionary figures is an elderly bespectacled Midwesterner whose conversation is liberally sprinkled with "my goshes" and "by golly's"—not the kind of talk one expects from a world-shaker. Carl Rogers is, nonetheless, one of the most important social revolutionaries of our time. He is the father of the human potential movement and is arguably the world's most influential living psychologist. If the name of Carl Rogers is not a household word to you, it may be because, true to his philosophy, Rogers tends to play the role of an enhancer or, to use his own favorite term, a "facilitator." His job as he conceives it is to bring out the best in you, to provide the accepting climate in which your undeveloped potentials can emerge, to supply, in his own words, "a psychological amniotic fluid."

He seems content to remain in the background, an unassuming figure of encouragement and support. Yet, there is hardly an American alive who hasn't been bathed in the amniotic fluid of human potentialism. Book shelves across the country are stocked with self-help and popular psychology manuals that are merely variations on themes that Rogers developed in books such as *Client Centered Therapy, On Becoming a Person, Freedom to Learn,* and *Carl Rogers on Encounter Groups.* Likewise, in recent years a number of magazines dedicated to the propositions of growth psychology have entered the market. Typical of these is *Self,* a sister of *Vogue* and *Mademoiselle,* and billed as "a new magazine for the woman who hasn't stopped growing." Popular TV programs such as "The Phil Donahue Show" display a clear bias toward the human potential agenda, as do such diverse groups as the NEA and SIECUS.

Beyond that, the language of professional caring that Rogers pioneered has become imbedded in everyday conversation. Terms such as "whole person," "awareness," "potentials," "growth," "self-concept," "realness," "spontaneity," and "process" have become staples of the vocabulary we use to describe personal states. More than any other individual, Rogers is responsible for the popularity of such concepts. Rogers was really the first psychologist (as long ago as 1940) who gave written permission for the rest of us to be completely free, to be the persons we were meant to be, to grow according to our own inner patterns. And more than anyone, as former Esalen director Richard Farson has observed, "he made psychology the business of normal people and normal people the business of psychology."

In 1973, in an address to the American Psychological Association, Rogers gave a modest accounting of the impact his work had had:

> It turned the field of counseling upside down. It opened psychotherapy to public scrutiny and research investigation. It has made possible the empirical study of highly subjective phenomena. It has helped to bring some change in the methods of education at every level. It has been one of the factors bringing change in concepts of industrial (and even military) leadership, of social work practice, of nursing practice, and of religious work. It has been responsible for one of the major trends in the encounter group movement. It has, in small ways at least, affected the philosophy of science. It is beginning to have some influence in interracial and intercultural relationships. It has even influenced students of theology and philosophy.

Then, a little later on, he added:

> To me as I try to understand the phenomenon, it seems that without knowing it I had expressed an idea whose time had come . . . as though a liquid solution had become supersatu-

rated, so that the addition of one tiny crystal initiated the formation of crystals throughout the whole mass.

This listing tends toward understatement. It is altogether too humble—too humble in the sense that the scope of his impact is much broader and goes much deeper than his assessment would indicate; too humble in the sense that Rogers professes to have played only a part in the unfolding drama while it could be argued that he has written much of the script.

That one phrase, "turned the field of counseling upside down," is telling. For the field of counseling is, in a sense, the paradigm for the whole culture. Philip Rieff, an eminent sociologist and social historian, states that ours is the age in which the therapeutic has triumphed over all other modes of cultural and personal organization. Rieff gives the credit to Freud, but it was Rogers's work that made it possible for all Americans to taste the food that previously only an elite had dined on. Rogers's is the much more democratic version of the therapeutic. Given some of the recent criticism of the therapeutic mentality, however, one wonders who would want to take credit for its triumph. It has become associated with self-indulgence—the me generation that Tom Wolfe parodied, and the narcissism that Christopher Lasch lashed out at. So just as Rogers's work can be applauded as a catalyst to liberation, it can also be attacked as a spur to excess.

What sort of work is it? Exactly what business has Rogers been about these many years? To free people from their ruts? To make them more feeling, more self-aware, more caring? Well, yes. But it doesn't stop there. Rogers goes well beyond that. He is frankly interested in the creation of a new type of human being, a new and better strain of human nature, a person as different from our present race as we are different from Australopithecus africanus. He is quite literal about this and quite determined. To fail to recognize this radical motif is to completely misread him. It is equivalent to reading Jefferson and concluding that the man was mainly interested in the pursuit of happiness. Here are some sample thoughts of the man whom Farson calls "the quiet revolutionary":

"I believe," writes Rogers, "that in our decaying culture we see the dim outlines of a new growth, of a new revolution, of a culture of a sharply different sort. I see that revolution as coming not in some great organized movement, not in a gun-carrying army with banners, not in manifestos and declarations, but through the emergence of a new kind of person, thrusting up through the dying, yellowing, putrifying leaves and stalks of our fading institutions." This "new mutant" will "change the fundamental nature of our society," and so Rogers concludes (in the articles from which these quotes are taken), "I simply say with all my heart: power to the emerging person and the revolution he carries within."

These are not the meanderings of an undisciplined idealist, but the culmination of forty years of practice and reflection. Rogers is not an eccentric like Wilhelm Reich or a flash-in-the-pan like Charles Reich. He is a past president of the American Psychological Association and the recipient of its first Distinguished Professional Contribution Award. He was the first person to establish a practicum in clinical psychology as a part of academic training, the first person to use the word "client" to substitute for "patient," the first psychologist to attack the Freudian concept of interpretation, the founder of the prestigious Center for Studies of the Person, the first president of the American Association for Applied Psychology, a director of counseling services for the USO, and a recipient of the 1967 Distinguished Contribution Award of the American Pastoral Counselors Association. His books, which have sold in the millions, have been translated into a dozen languages. A documentary film on his work won an Academy Award. When a fitting opponent was sought to confront B. F. Skinner in a series of debates, Rogers was the obvious choice. He is the founder of the nondirective (sometimes called client-centered) school of therapy—the most widely used of all counseling techniques. The spread of the encounter group movement probably owes more to Rogers than to any other single individual; so does the spread of liberal ideas about schooling in the sixties and seventies. Partly because of Rogers and his popularizers, our ideas about marriage have been profoundly changed. And then, of course, there's the women's movement: Rogers's psychology primed the pump for sex-role liberation and provided a repertoire of words and concepts in which it could be framed.

In view of his radical ideas and in view of the sweep of his influence, a good case can be made that Rogers is one of the key figures in the intellectual history of the last twenty-five years. The fascinating thing about intellectual history, however, is that at some point it comes down from the level of intellect and starts walking around in the streets, occasionally bumping into people and even knocking them down. Locke was intellectual history until the Battle of Lexington Green; Marx was intellectual history until the October Revolution; Thoreau was intellectual history until the British were forced out of India. Of equal interest is the way in which ideas once translated into social change take on entirely unexpected shapes and forms. From time to time in the course of intellectual history, the bread that is cast upon the waters comes back moldy. We are now beginning to feel the repercussions of the Rogerian revolution on our society. But what accounts for that greenish tinge around the edge of culture? Is it simply mold, as his critics claim, or is it, as his supporters believe, the sprouting of new and verdant life?

Tonight Dr. Rogers is giving a seminar on "Humanistic Education." Apparently it's a favor for a friend, because the setting is the basement playroom of a private house with scarcely room for twenty-five people. The "fee" for the seminar is five dollars, which is quite modest considering that, as one woman in the room puts it, "This must have been what it was like for those students at Clark." She's referring to the fact that Sigmund Freud in 1909 delivered a landmark series of lectures at Clark University in Worcester, Massachusetts. She is perceptive enough to realize that the Clark lectures were an altogether different kind of event. The parallel she means to draw is that we also are privileged to be in the presence of a history-making man. When the story of psychology comes to be written from some future perspective, it will be seen that although Freud got people thinking about their inner lives, it wasn't until Rogers and his popularizers that people at large began to do something about it.

The comparison between Rogers and Freud is also justi-fied for another reason. Therapeutic psychology has evolved into three main forces: the Freudians, the behaviorists, and the hu-manists. And Rogers is certainly the most prominent figure in that third force. The "Third Force" is a term the humanists have long used to describe themselves. Moreover, they have a solemn, almost reverential way of speaking about it. "The Third Force"—on the lips of a potentialist, it sounds like a line from *Star Wars*: "the Force surrounds us, penetrates us, it binds the universe together." Third Forcers definitely feel bound together by some mysterious energy which only seems to work for you if you believe in it. But if you allow the force to work through you, it constitutes an immense power for good. When these people talk about being "energized," they mean a good deal more than what is commonly conveyed in the phrase "I feel energetic."

"This must have been what it was like for those students at Clark." The woman repeats her assertion to a new listener. Meanwhile, a buzz of excitement fills the room. Rogers hasn't entered yet. People are introducing themselves, getting to know each other. There also appears to be a bit of entrepreneurial activity going on. On each of the metal folding chairs a yellow leaflet announces the following:

The Growth Centre

The Growth Centre is in the process of Becoming. I want to match your needs with what I have to offer. I invite you to share your needs, wants, and ideas both personally and professionally. So that I may respond to you personally, please include your name, address and telephone number.

The leaflet is the creation, not of Rogers, but of the hostess, who happens also to be a therapist. Not to be outdone, another person, a handsome middle-aged man in a white leisure suit, is confidently introducing himself: "Hi! I'm Sam Strong" (or something like that), "I do death counseling," and he's handing out green leaflets describing his services.

All in all, though, it's an average looking set of upper middle-class Americans: a group of mellow travelers. The only unusual thing is the eyes. Several people in the group have a wide-eyed look that is a strange combination of innocence, intensity, and expectation. They don't blink or shift their glance. It is the kind of stare that seems to demand more than business as usual.

Rogers enters unobtrusively, wearing grey flannel slacks and a muted orchid-design Hawaiian shirt. He is a healthy looking seventy-five years old, almost completely bald. His head inclines forward at a permanent angle, the result perhaps of years spent hunching forward to better hear his clients (most of his life has been spent as a practicing psychotherapist). His eyes are magnified by thick glasses, which could account for the fact that Rogers always appears to be peering intently at you. It's a look of concern though, not aggression. His smile also shows concern. It's not the practiced smile of the fellow who wants to convince you of his sincerity, but a kindly smile. He is the picture of a kind and patient grandfather. He also has a habit of nodding his head up and down, up and down ever so slightly when someone else is talking, as if to say "uh huh, uh huh, I'm listening intently to you. I understand what it is that concerns

135

you." A caricaturist, noting the baldness and the head, which is almost too small for the body, inclined forward and bobbing up and down, and the wide thin smile, and the beaklike nose, might be tempted to sketch Rogers as a large and gentle turtle. But he is a turtle who has long since come out of his shell, one in whom trust has replaced character armor.

Right now he's talking to a couple of women in the front seats. "Tell me about yourselves," he says. He looks so interested and expectant that they can't help but tell. After this he starts moving around the room from person to person, his head nodding in empathy. "Tell me about yourself." Somehow the analogy with Freud begins to weaken.

Rogers's wandering about the room seems to have a confusing effect on one young man. "I wonder what the format will be?" he whispers to another. The older man smiles knowingly. Format? The boy is obviously an initiate. There will be no format tonight.

The hostess, a well-dressed woman in her midthirties, now calls for a moment of silent meditation, "to bring together our energies." "I'd like you to close your eyes," she says, "and go back to that moment when you first heard that Dr. Rogers would be here tonight. Simply allow yourself to be in that place. Let your tape run. Be in touch with your expectations of tonight . . . (long, long pause) . . . and when you feel ready to be here now, just come back to the room and open your eyes."

The sacred character of the event is established at that moment. This is not simply a seminar—it has already acquired the atmosphere of a prayer meeting. Something more than education is in the air.

The hostess continues, "It's always very special to be with Carl, but what this something is is always intangible. And it seems to me that I thought that way until very recently when I became in touch with what it really is—it is your tremendous acceptance of another human being. It's a rare experience in the world to experience that among people."

"It touches me," says Rogers. Then he begins. At the start he makes it clear, although in a nondirective way, that the discussion doesn't have to stay in any set range: "This is your seminar, and you can do anything you want with it." Then he begins to talk at random about how he discovered that in therapy his clients could be trusted to find healthy directions for themselves, and how he later discovered that students could also take charge of their education, and how he has learned to trust his own deep instincts and those of other persons. He tells of his recent trip to Brazil, where he helped lead a massive encounter of some eight hundred people. Somehow or other they got those eight hundred people together in a big circle. "We're still trying to figure out how we did it," he says. But one thing he is certain of. "We were all deeply in touch." Several exclamations of awe follow this revelation. The incongruity of mass intimacy does not seem to strike anyone.

Rogers speaks with a broad, gentle, Midwestern accent. His conversation has a rural flavor—not just folksy, but almost boyish and innocent in its enthusiasm. For emphasis he favors exclamation of the "my golly" variety. But along with the youthful earnestness there is often a youthful vagueness. He finishes up his description of the giant circle "ten or twelve deep" in Brazil with the rather unsatisfactory though tantalizing observation that "things happened there that you just wouldn't believe."

Dr. Rogers has a mental reserve of statistics and research studies to back his theories, but he obviously prefers to relate grass-root testimonials and endorsements. "It's interesting," he says. "I had a letter just a few days ago from a woman who was in one of our groups . . ." And again the room takes on that church-meeting atmosphere. Somehow one is reminded of a radio preacher—the kind who says, "I had a letter the other day from a woman in Memphis who had suffered from rheumatism for thirty years until she put her life in the hands of the Lord Jesus!" Rogers is quite low-key in comparison with the average media evangelist, but he recognizes the importance of the personal testimony in inspiring faith. Letters from thankful follow-ers are a mainstay of all his recent books.

"Why don't I throw it open at this point. Let me know where you're at."

Where they're at is this: most of those present are teach-ers or are in some helping profession. They are trying to use humanistic approaches, but are being frustrated by "the admin-istration" and beyond that "the establishment." The word "sub-versive" keeps coming up. "You almost have to be subversive in order to be humanistic," says one of the teachers.

Even though humanistic psychology is the most popular branch of psychology, even though Rogers's philosophy has be-come the common wisdom among the educated and the educa-tors, humanists still think of themselves as a beleagured minor-ity, lonely revolutionaries carrying on the work of The Force against overwhelming odds. Much of the driving power of the movement seems to stem from the ability of its leaders to con-vince their followers that they are challenging the Fates, that they are the underground, and that everyone else is either a Nazi or a mindless collaborator.

They're looking to Rogers now for something solid, some weapon to bring into battle against the administrators and au-thoritarians of their world. But Rogers is nondirective to the core.

"I'm wondering," says one young woman, "about this question of humanistic approaches on the one hand and bureau-cratic realities on the other. What's the gap, and how do you bridge the gap?"

"How do you see that?"

"That's why I asked you."

"But you seem to have given a great deal of thought to this."

Well, he's got her there. You might as well ask Socrates for a straight answer as ask Rogers. This is not evasion, however; it's perfectly consistent with his philosophy of nondirectiveness, and it squares with his belief that each person carries within herself a health-seeking force. Rogers won't let her put the responsibility on him, not when, if she only knew it, all the answers to her problems lie within her, waiting for the unfolding. The facilitator can provide the acceptance, but you have to do your own un-folding.

Something's wrong, however, something that wouldn't have come up in the early days of the encounter group move-ment. From their comments, from the jargon they use, it is plain that many of these people have been involved in the movement for years. They *have* been unfolding, they *have* been aware; for years they've been getting in touch with their feelings. Yet, things still aren't working for them. Some narrow-gauge bureau-crat can still throw them off the track. One man tells of a particularly truculent school board member who seems to hover like a shadow over his dreams and schemes for liberating the students in his class.

This time Rogers has a straight answer. "If we could get that school councilor into a three- or four-day encounter group, all kinds of things would change." There is no trace of doubt in Rogers's voice as he says this. And there are murmurs of approv-al from others in the group. *If we could get that school councilor into a three- or four-day encounter group . . . he'd have to see the light then.* There seems to be a general agreement that this indeed is the answer.

Exactly what would happen to this benighted school board member once bundled off to a weekend encounter is left to the imagination. Presumably that rigid character armor would come unfastened. He would find that he doesn't need it any longer; he would find that people accept him for what he is, in all his naked vulnerability. And pretty soon things would begin to change: sensitive, student-centered teachers would emerge from the woodwork, open classrooms would flourish, encounter grouping would take the place of physical education. That, or something like it, seems to be the implication of Rogers's solution.

Get the man into a weekend marathon. Rogers truly believes this. For him, the encounter group process holds the key to unlocking every door—from stuffy marriages to racial tension. He sees it as the paradigm for all social relationships (and international relations as well). Such sweeping notions leave him, of course, open to charges of simplistic thinking. His friend and colleague Richard Farson once wrote of him, "By and large he is unable to recognize either the coexistence of opposites or the enormous complexity of human affairs."

Those complexities are hovering all around the room tonight, but they haven't come to roost just yet. Meanwhile Rogers has warmed up to this group. He wants to head them away from mundane job concerns and back to the wonders of their inner world:

"I guess I've become more aware of the fact that it's personal presence that accomplishes things—whatever I mean by that, and that can be analyzed too perhaps, but I'm not sure that it will ever be. I guess I've moved away a little from the intellectual approach to a more subjective, holistic approach. I realize if change is going to happen, one person has to be present to another. . . ."

This seems to strike a responsive chord. One fellow in the back row who has apparently seen through the vagueness to the inner truth sums it up:

"I thought that there was an—an additive—that I was very excited about what you said about personal presence—uh—that captures it."

There are many nods and grunts of approval. "Personal presence"—that captures it!

Even if there is precious little content to these observations, they still sound right. The use of words like "holistic," "change," and "person" cover a multitude of nebulousities. In *Language and Silence* George Steiner suggests that for many people today the function of language is not so much to communicate as it is to provide a soothing backdrop to life, in much the same way that music does. Just as we look for certain types of music to confirm and expand our mood, we also look for a type of conversation that will confirm or heighten our mood. The human potential sound seems to blend particularly well with the current mood.

Rogers continues: "Let me ask kind of a last question: Are there things that poeple are wondering about or thinking about or questions that you'd like to raise but that you feel, 'well, it doesn't seem quite appropriate to the way the discussion is going' or something? Because I think that those are the kind of things that would be very valuable to bring up. Only people feel, 'here's something I'd like to bring up, only it doesn't seem appropriate to ask him now, I'd like to ask him after the meeting.' But it would be a good thing to ask me at the meeting."

At last. This, it seems, is what the group has been waiting for all along: permission to talk about themselves. There are a few ice-breakers at first. One gentleman—the death counselor—says he's been wondering where the men's room is. This brings a wave of laughter. That laughter, though, is just the opening that Irwin needs.

Irwin is a thin man in his late thirties with big mournful eyes and moist pink lips showing through his beard. There is a catch in his voice as he speaks. He's holding back a tide of emotion.

"You were talking—about—why—humanistic education can't work—and I was feeling that it can't work because people don't want it to, and I was looking around and I was feeling unhappy, and I was looking around and everybody else seems happy—'cause I'm unhappy (at this point several sympathetic voices try to reassure Irwin that they're not happy either). I'm sitting in rows, I'm way back here. When I first heard about the meeting I said, 'I hear there might be a chance to meet Carl Rogers.' "

He wants, apparently, more than a chance to hear Rogers speak. A handshake and a greeting are not what he has in mind either. He is seeking some sort of communion with Rogers. But Rogers will not be cast in the role of messiah. He says nothing.

Not everyone realizes at first that this is a cry for help on Irwin's part. Ginny, a plump middle-aged lady wearing bangs and an Indian print dress, thinks he's unsatisfied with the seating arrangement. "Could we maybe fold up our chairs and sit on the floor?" she asks.

But this is not Irwin's complaint. "No," he says, "I don't think that being real and in touch and human is always a necessity, 'cause looking around it seems that everybody seems quite happy—you know with the information, the studies, I didn't find anything of personal interest until the question, you know, 'what are you doing with your life?' Carl, that's what I wanted to ask you. I wanted to tell you some of my struggles, but this isn't appropriate, you know—the others came here to get information."

Rogers's response is thoughtful, sensitive: "Would you try? You know, perhaps the others feel exactly the same way you do. Would you like to share a little bit?"

"Well, O.K. I saw a poem today. I was waiting in a waiting room today, and I read a poem, and I liked it and I asked the woman if I could make a copy on a thermofax, and I, uh, it, uh, touched me. Maybe it will touch other people. Want to hear a poem?"

"Yes! Yes!" says the group.

"Everybody didn't say they wanted to hear a poem, see— I don't know . . ."

"Yes, we do!" replies the chorus.

"Maybe you don't want to. You didn't come here to listen to me read a poem. I just had a birthday, maybe that's one of those bits . . ." He trails off. "Richard Eberhart, Class of '26, Dartmouth, 1930-76. It's called 'If I Could Only Live at the Pitch That Is Near Madness.' Then he reads the entire poem:

If I could only live at the pitch that is near madness
When everything is as it was in my childhood
Violent, vivid, and of infinite possibility:
That the sun and the moon broke over my head.

Then I cast time out of the trees and fields,
Then I stood immaculate in the Ego:
Then I eyed the world with all delight,
Reality was the perfection of my sight.

And time has big handles on the hands,
Fields and trees a way of being themselves.
I saw battalions of the race of mankind
Standing stolid, demanding a moral answer.

I gave the moral answer and I died
And into a realm of complexity came
Where nothing is possible but necessity
And the truth wailing there like a red babe.

Irwin's voice quavers as he reads it, but the proper drama and phrasing is there. It is a fascinating poem, and it fairly captures the essence of human potentialism: the worship of the child and the innocent state of nature that the child represents, the wish to return to the state of childhood, the desire for "infinite possibility" or unlimited potentials, the casting out of time, the desire to live in some unending summer free from the ravages of time, the fear of the limitations that might be imposed by the passage of time or the demands of moral duty.

When he finally finishes, there are murmurs of approval.

"I appreciate your sharing this," says Rogers.

"Thank you," says Ginny.

"Thank you," says another.

"I appreciate your sharing where you're at," says Bernice.

143

All this openness prompts others to share. Bill, a man in his thirties with a Vista-volunteer look about him, tells his own story: "I guess when I heard him read that poem I kind of felt, uh, a kind of excitement for life that you're talking about in the child. I had that, like four years ago . . ." And he pours out his story. Only he's lost it now—that childlike excitement. He had a wife and three children then, but he's divorced now and saddled with support payments, and yet he never gets to see his children. The man looks beaten.

"My father just had a massive stroke." The voice belongs to a woman, possibly forty years old, who has been quiet up to now. She's trying to find a home for him. She tells the whole sad story.

Bill is sympathetic. He knows how hard it is to keep up one's spirits under such crushing blows. "I guess I really tried to use the humanistic approach—uh, in the, uh, situation I just described—and—I guess I feel it was the right thing to do; not that I did it all that well. I don't know, it just really takes something out of you."

"One of the fascinating things in what I heard you say," responds Rogers, "is, I can easily imagine you saying, 'I tried the humanistic approach and it failed, so it's no damn good.' And instead you're saying, 'and I wish I could get back to more of it.' That's really good!"

Bill nods, but the look on his face suggests that Rogers has missed the point. Bernice hasn't though. "What really touched me, Bill," she says, "is you used the word 'regaining' before. There seem to be certain things that I somehow feel that I'm never going to get back. It seems to me in the years that I've tried to pick up the pieces since I was divorced a lot of things seem to be picked up on the outside in my life, but deep inside me there seem to be certain things that I'm never going to get back again—like trusting and loving."

Irwin, who first headed the group off on this somber tack, knows exactly what they're talking about. He's still wondering what became of his child's garden of delights: "For me, it's the innocence that's lost. Not the sense of loving or wanting to love. But the feeling there's no innocence as in childhood—that no matter what you do to recreate that love and spontaneity, it's gone."

What's happening, of course, is that at least half the people in this room are hovering around what has popularly come to be known as the midlife crisis. They are old enough now to see their parents dying or dependent or simply depleted by the passage of time. Time is catching up with them as well, slowing them down. They've already had their marriages and children and divorces; their careers are well underway. But the main thing is this: they've tried freedom and spontaneity and openness, and it really hasn't gotten them anywhere. At least not to the nirvana they were expecting. They feel that they've been treading water. Fatigue is setting in; age is catching up with them. It casts a pterodactyl-like shadow over their lives.

Along with death and dying, the midlife crisis has become a lively topic in psychology these days. Psychologists and journalists are busy charting the waters of midlife, pinpointing the sandbars, shoals, submerged wrecks, and riptides of aging. In Gail Sheehy's *Passages,* one can read about the "Catch 30's," the "Forlorn 40's," and the "Refurbished 50's." *Passages,* however, is only the most popular of these Gesell-for-the-graying manuals. In the same bookstores one can find *Shifting Gears, The Middle-Age Crisis, The Male Mid-Life Crisis, Looking Ahead (A Woman's Guide to the Problems and Joys of Growing Older),* and the more serious studies of Gould, Valiant, and Levinson.

Still, despite the attention it's now getting, the midlife crisis comes as quite a shock. It wasn't supposed to happen, least of all to these people. The implicit promise of all the earlier joy and growth books was that life would be a continual "up" for those who had the simple intelligence and goodwill to master a few self-actualizing techniques. There would be pain and risk, of course, but you only grow by risking. The important thing to know is that you can take charge of your life. There are proven ways. If you could only learn to get in touch with the "wisdom of your body" (or whatever), you could surf right over life's miseries. Your life would be an endless summer.

Only it seems not to have worked—not for a lot of people in this room. They've tried encountering, they've been open to their experience, they are self-aware, they have gotten in touch with their inner selves. But where in the name of Fritz Perls is this *joy* they're supposed to have? And they're getting tired. If they gave in to the wisdom of their bodies at this point, they might just sleep all the time. They know that pain is involved in growth, but who in his wildest imaginings would have predicted this much pain?

Rogers, however, won't admit that there are existential limitations out there that may not only impede actualization, but stop it dead. Instead, his prescription for these people in pain is the same one he's been suggesting for years in his books: take more risks. He says, "I don't feel so much older as long as I keep on taking risks, and that has been a very valuable learning experience for me." This idea of growing by taking risks occurs over and over in the writings of Rogers. It fits in nicely with his pictures of himself as an experimenter. But, unlike his adversary B. F. Skinner, Rogers does not confine his experiments to pigeons and white rats. He takes the whole field of human relationships for his laboratory. Encounter groups, of which Rogers has personally led hundreds, are considered to be miniature laboratories in human relations. Moreover, in his numerous and influential books and articles Rogers frankly encourages his readers to be experimental in their approach to other persons. At one point in *Becoming Partners,* Rogers advocated an "R and D" approach to relationships because it has worked so well in modern industry.

Typically, however, the risks that Rogers and his popularizers encourage are not the risks involved in making commitments, but the risks involved in getting out of commitments, which in the Newspeak of psychology is called "change" or "growth." The basic risk is to attempt to be yourself, or more accurately, the person you were meant to be. If the struggle brings you into collision with others or drives you away from them—well, that's a chance you have to take. It's a courageous thing to be oneself. Others will misunderstand you or even hate you. But you will be no good to others unless you are one with yourself. Only then can you allow them to be themselves.

Still, there are these people in this basement room struggling with the midlife blues, who by their own admission have been cut off from spouses, children, parents, colleagues, and their own childhood innocence—not, one assumes, out of timidity, but more likely as a direct result of their risk taking. And it begins to look as though what they need is not risks but roots. If they had roots, after all, why would they be here seeking solace from strangers? Why are they drawing an interest of frustration from a principle of actualization?

A British sociologist, Stanislav Andreski, suggested ten years ago that social scientists, particularly psychologists, have helped create the kind of society that makes psychologists indispensable. They are like firemen, he said, who arrive at the scene of a blaze and begin to pump oil on it. Here is this roomful of unhappy citizens looking to Dr. Rogers for help, and the impious thought occurs: what if this man from whom they are seeking solutions is the one who gave them their problems in the first place? What if the prescription is exacerbating the disease? Could it be that Rogers and others like him have raised their hopes beyond all possibility of fulfillment? What if human nature is not all that malleable?

Even an ardent Rogers admirer like Farson can spot the problem. He observes of Rogers, "By raising our expectations, he has also given us a new level of discontent. The discrepancy between what people are ordinarily *able* to make happen in their relationships and what they have come to believe is *possible* to make happen as a result, say, of reading a book by Carl Rogers, is the cause of much disruption in their lives."

The result of reading a book by Carl Rogers is that you come away thinking that just about anything and everything is possible. You had always hoped this were true, that you could have your cake and eat it too, that you could simultaneously, for example, have deep, meaningful relationships with as many people as you could schedule into your calender. After reading Rogers, you come to think that perhaps it is possible. He seems to understand about all those unexercised potentials lying fallow within, and, most appealing, he seems to suggest that they are the best part of you: the natural, sensitive, spontaneous, ambisexual, supple, innocent, curious, childlike center of self. Reading Rogers gives you a paternal and protective feeling for this neglected orphan within. You realize that you've been limiting yourself, that you were meant for a wider, more varied life, that you haven't been doing yourself justice. And then the revolutionary messages begin to sink in: "Why not liberate yourself?" "You have so much to give." "Become the self you were meant to be." This will necessarily involve risks, but growth only comes through risking. And imagine what a revelation for others it will be when they gaze on your true self stripped of society's encrustations.

Reading Rogers is a secular invitation to be born again. Rogers's students used to refer to his book *On Becoming a Person* as "the Bible." You can easily see why. It is both inspirational and humble: humble in the presence of the self. In this secular religion, being born again does not mean receiving the Spirit or "putting on Christ." Rather, it means being baptized in the fluid waters of your own self. Who needs a God above when there is one within? The self, according to Rogers, is, in its unlimited potential, virtually a god. The most sublime sacrament is then the actualization of self. So widespread has this belief become that many people can no longer frame an answer to the question of life's purpose except in terms of their own self-development. But perhaps the most interesting corollary to a religious life, and the one with the most practical implications, is this: just as the true disciple of Christ is exhorted to leave father or mother or wife or children and "come, follow me," so also the true seeker after self may have to cut his ties. It is not Christ that he follows, of course, nor Carl Rogers; it is his own inner voice that says, "come, follow me." For the original disciples, this "leave all others and follow me" was perhaps the biggest stumbling-block of all. For the modern devotee of self, it is perhaps one of the main attractions, since it offers a justification for getting out of relationships that are seen as growth-limiting. In the upside-down religion of potentialism, even divorce can be looked upon as a sacred duty. One of the participants in the seminar puts it this way: "There have been lots of endings in my life, a marriage and an intensive counselor training experience . . . and I feel as if I'm being born and being born and being born again."

Apparently it was no mistake to start the seminar with a meditation. The prayer-group atmosphere is appropriate, for if human potentialism is not a religion, it is an excellent mimic of one. It is a particularly good mimic of Christianity, with the consequence that huge chunks of humanistic psychology have been imported wholesale into Christian churches and schools. Droves of nuns, priests, ministers, and laymen have been busy translating Christian ideas into spirit and forms that are unmistakably Rogerian—sometimes with direct aid from Rogers himself. In 1967, for instance, Rogers and his colleagues at the Western Behavioral Science Institute were invited by the Immaculate Heart Order of Nuns to revitalize their extensive school system in the Los Angeles area. For the next two years the system, which included the Immaculate Heart College, several high schools, and a string of elementary schools, became the scene of intensive encounter and marathon group activity. One has to go back to the appearance of the devils in the convent of

Loudun to find a more radical transformation of a group of Sisters. Within a short time the nuns had become humanized, feminized, and revolutionized. Not long after the departure of the WBSI people they cut their ties with the official Catholic Church.

William Coulson, one of the project leaders, later wrote: "When we started the project . . . there were six hundred nuns and fifty-nine schools: a college, eight high schools, and fifty elementary schools. Now, four years later as I write, a year following the formal completion of the project, there are two schools left and no nuns." Afterwards it was argued that these things would have happened anyway given the times and the conservative nature of the Church in the City of Angels, but Rogers's presence seems a large coincidence.

Something more than coincidence seems to be at work, however, in a religious education series put out by Holt, Rinehart, and Winston for Catholic high school students. The authors handle the section on the sacrament of marriage by excerpting five pages from Rogers's book *Becoming Partners: Marriage and Its Alternatives*. By comparison, two sentences in the discussion section at the end of the chapter are devoted to Christ and his views on marriage. Other religious education series (they are no longer called catechisms) are laced with human-potential sentiment. The religious education series for Catholic grade schoolers put out by Benziger Brothers Publishers starts off in Book One with the question "Who am I?" and replies, "I am me, I am special," and then goes on to say, "All boys and girls are good and special," and "all children have feelings. It's all right to have feelings." Book Eight concludes with the reminder that creation does not end until it has "reached its fullest potential."

There are other indications that of the many unusual changes now taking place in Catholicism, not all have been inspired by Vatican II. For example, in a 1975 survey a population of former nuns gave "inability to be me" as a major reason for leaving the convent. In Quincy, Massachusetts, a nun tells a group of two hundred that "parents don't have the right to talk to children about sin." Instead, she urges parents to learn about "values clarification"—a set of techniques based on Rogerian principles. In many Catholic parishes now, despite an explicit prohibition from the Vatican, children are given first communion before first confession. The warrant for this practice is not to be found in theology but, once again, in the humanistic notion that children are just naturally good and therefore don't have anything to confess. Instances of this sort are common in the Catholic Church and in liberal Protestant churches too. These days they are much more the rule than the exception.

It is a strange irony that Rogers, who long ago disavowed Christianity, has since had such a profound effect on it. He began his career of helping people by entering Union Theological Seminary in the hope of becoming a minister, and actually assumed the position of pastor in a rural Vermont parish one summer in 1925 as part of his training. But a year later he left Union for Columbia University across the street, and a career in psychology. Since then he has had no kind words for Christianity. In fact, the characteristics of "The emerging person . . . run strongly counter to the orthodoxies and dogmas of the major Western religions." Nevertheless, his theory has a strong appeal for Christians. Even if Rogers is avowedly not a Christian, his philosophy seems to echo many Christian themes—not merely broad themes of loving and trusting, but more specific ones such as the idea, very appealing to charismatics and evangelicals, that personal experience is the ultimate appeal from every question; or the idea that the letter of the law kills while the spirit gives life; or the idea that we should not judge others; or the idea that the path of wisdom is to become like little children.

Getting in touch with the child within is high on the list of human potential priorities. Such an idea is bound to be popular with people who have a Christian background. Actually, however, Rogers's version of the idea has nothing to do with the

Christian one because he starts from a different premise. His philosophical fondness for children is based on the assumption that children are somehow closer to the state of nature. And natural instincts, Rogers firmly believes, can be trusted. Accordingly, the closer you get to a childlike state, the healthier you become. This is the context in which Irwin's birthday prompts him to focus on a poem about lost childhood innocence.

Here, of course, the religious parallel breaks down. Christianity is based on the fundamental premise that man is a fallen creature (corrupt from his birth, according to the Old Testament). His salvation lies not in expressing his natural self, but in being rescued from it; we can only avoid evil with the help of external rules (such as the Ten Commandments) and can receive salvation only with the aid of divine grace. Children, moreover, are as deeply implicated in the original sin as adults. We are to become like them not because they are naturally good, but because being still capable of awe, they are still capable of humility.

Curiously enough, the religious view is partially echoed in the writings of Sigmund Freud, who, despite his religious iconoclasm, was deeply pessimistic about the natural state. In the Freudian view it is society, working through the agency of the superego, that keeps individuals civilized. For Rogers, it is the exact opposite. We are naturally good; society corrupts us. In asserting this belief, Rogers lays claim to a major American tradition. Americans have always had a soft spot in their heart for the "noble savage." It is a favorite political and literary theme, and one which permeates our attitude toward children. W. H. Auden remarked in one of his essays that the child hero in American literature is "a Noble Savage, and anarchist. . . . His heroic virtue—that is to say, his superiority to adults—lies in his freedom from conventional ways of thinking and acting: Social habits, from manners to creeds, are regarded as false or hypocritical or both."

Child heroes in English literature, on the contrary, are

always trying to carry on the civilized English traditions of justice and fair play under the most bizarre and anarchic conditions. In C. S. Lewis's Narnia stories, the charm of the child heroes lies in their ability to transplant typical English virtues to completely alien soil. Likewise, in *Alice in Wonderland* rational, organized society equals sanity. For Alice, according to Auden, "Wonderland and Looking-Glass Land are fun to visit, but no places to live in. Even when she is there, Alice can ask herself with some nostalgia 'if anything would ever happen in a natural way again,' and by 'natural' she means the opposite of what Rousseau would mean. She means peaceful, civilized society."

The English view is captured nicely in Yeats "A Prayer for my Daughter" when he says,

> How but in custom and in ceremony
> Are innocence and beauty born?
> Ceremony's a name for the rich horn,
> And custom for the spreading laurel tree.

In short, it is society which by its rituals and traditions protects, indeed creates, the innocence of children. It is not, however, the *socialized* child that Irwin and the others seem to mourn. What they want back is the irrepressible, free-spirited child-of-nature, unhampered by conventions and still alive—somewhere deep within.

But human potentialism is a supple and fluid stream of ideas. Anyone who focused too closely on the child homage aspect of it might not be prepared for what happens next. Out of the blue, the death counselor brings up the subject of child pornography. Perhaps one of the earlier comments about childhood beauty and innocence has triggered off a chain of associations in his mind. Angry but controlled, he recites a catalog of the evils involved. He is outraged over the whole sordid phenomenon, and he wants Rogers to share his indignation: "I'm certainly very, very pessimistic about the moral disintegration of our society. I'm just wondering how you feel about those kinds of monumental outrages that we're beginning to see?"

There is a long pause before Rogers replies. "I'm reluctant to generalize on that because—uh—it seems like such a many-faceted thing—uh—certainly I go along with your feeling of outrage about that particular thing, but—uh—I wouldn't want to generalize about whether we're morally worse-off or better-off than we were a generation ago."

When Rogers says, "Certainly I go along with your feeling of outrage about that particular thing," it sounds almost parenthetical and somehow unconvincing—like a government bureaucrat saying, "Certainly we'll do everything we can to help."

Rogers can't really say much of anything because he's already gone on record (in a 1975 interview with Richard Evans) against all pornography laws. Beyond that, he is philosophically committed to a completely nonjudgmental approach toward persons. It is the foundation, in fact, on which his nondirective counseling technique is built. For Rogers, the freedom to be oneself takes precedence over every other claim. No one else can know what it's like to be you, let alone what directions in life you ought to take. Consequently, you shouldn't pay too much attention to what others think of you, and you, likewise, should avoid evaluating others. You should rather cultivate what Rogers calls "an internal locus of evaluation." In a complex moral situation the only question to ask is this: "what would actualize me, and what would unactualize me by the experience?" This "internal evaluation" rule prevents Rogers from passing judgment on anyone except society at large. Besides, Rogers can see other sides to the question. This child pornography thing is a "many-faceted" subject. One imagines that it may involve the delicate question of attempting to impose limits on the exercise of an adult's sexual potentials—and, for that matter, on the child's natural instincts. Pedophiliacs as well as children have a need to fulfill themselves. And, from a human potential perspective, one can well appreciate their attraction to the guile-

154

less charms of the young. Evaluate not then, that you be not evaluated.

The death counselor is not prepared for such liberality or for such a hasty termination of the topic. He was expecting more, and now he appears flustered—at a loss for words. He knows that he has committed some sort of *faux pas;* he senses he has almost put Rogers into a corner. But it's evident by the puzzled look on his face that he doesn't have a clue what that corner is. To everyone's obvious relief, the whole subject is quickly and quietly dumped, and the group moves on to a discussion of "how we can give children more power in schools."

"Hate the sin and love the sinner," expresses a widely held Christian sentiment based on a belief in objective right and wrong. For Christians, it is even a duty of love to rebuke the sinner and call him to repent because he too ought to be able to see what is right. Humanistic theory, while all for loving the sinner, doesn't seem to allow for hating the sin, or even calling it sin. Who is to say what's right and wrong? That is the trouble with the authoritarians and the dogmatists: they think they have the right to impose their values on others. Rather, say Rogerians, everyone must choose his own values. In *Freedom to Learn,* Rogers's book on teaching, he states, ". . . it is the growing child and adolescent who must evaluate his own behaviors, come to his own conclusions, and decide on the standards which are appropriate for him." One corollary of this principle is that pupils in schools ought to evaluate and grade themselves. (Interestingly, Rogers's presentation is always true to his philosophy of nonimposition. All his statements of principle are qualified with remarks such as "Here are some thoughts of mine," "It seems to me," "Here are some learnings which have been useful to me.") During the sixties and early seventies many teachers, inspired by Rogers and writers such as John Holt, put pupil self-evaluation into practice by letting students grade themselves. Most abandoned the experiment, but the underlying hypothesis that a teacher doesn't have much of a right to judge his students lingered, and helped to boost the general grade inflation that still plagues education at all levels.

Still very much alive in the schools is another derivative of Rogerian nonjudgmentalism: values clarification. The technique was developed by psychologists Sidney Simon, Merrill Harmin, and Louis Raths, but in conception it is pure Rogers. Simon and his colleagues feel that the world's ills can be traced by-and-large to values confusion. The answer to this confusion is to help individuals clarify their values: not to arrive at a morality or come to conclusions about what is right or wrong—it is assumed that objective right and wrong do not exist—but to get in touch with one's own "valuing system." What you get in touch with is assumed to be reliable and trustworthy, a good guide for you, though, of course, not necessarily for anyone else. You can't impose your values on someone else, nor they on you. Although the values clarification approach has been gobbled up by a great many public schools and by many liberal Catholic and Protestant educators, it has raised a furor among the Moral Majority, and also among conservative Catholics and Jews who see it as a way of introducing values relativity while at the same time undermining traditional values and undoing the attempts of parents and churches to form character.

Rogers has always dismissed such complaints against humanistic psychology as tradition-bound. Despite his grandfatherly demeanor, he is a completely modern man who is interested in helping create even more modern men. When talking or writing about those who let the past or traditional authority guide them, he will often step out of his nonjudgmental shoes. Once at a university commencement address Rogers removed his cap and gown because "I want to speak to you as Carl Rogers, in 1969, not as a medieval symbol. So I hope I will not offend you if I remove these medieval trappings. . . ."

His attempts to stay abreast of the times have sometimes had, however, the effect of putting him in a ludicrous light. The observation that "he who marries the spirit of the age is soon a widower" is nowhere better illustrated than in a letter of complaint sent by Rogers in July 1968 to the board of directors of the Western Behavioral Science Institute. Along with the letter he enclosed a three-page story of his own compositon entitled "Camelot—A Fable Retold." Here is a sample:

> "I want to tell you cats something about a flick I seen a while ago—*Camelot*. They tell me some of the eggheads thought it was strictly from Dullsville. But not me. I thought it was groovy. I dig all this stuff about knights in armor and a king who is scared of getting hitched to some broad he's never seen, and fellows and their chicks tumbling in the flowers and having some fun doin' it—and a lot of other stuff. But I'm not going to try to tell you the whole story— I'm not *that* square!"

Rogers, who was on the point of resigning from WBSI, apparently thought that this kind of prose would have a powerful effect on the board (which included S. I. Hayakawa). It did not. It is instructive to note that Rogers normally writes in a clear and competent style, and in his unpublished "China Diary" (1922) shows literary promise. For example:

> As we got higher, the whole Foochow basin lay in a panorama below us—the long island, with a silver strip of river on each side—the bevy of dusty winged junks coming upriver on the incoming tide—the little clustered villages scattered over the plain, with a few wisps of smoke hanging over each one—the clean little rice paddies, cut here and there with little threadlike canals—and off to the right, the close packed city of Foochow, with a crowd of anchored junks at the river bank.

It is difficult to fathom the apparent lack of judgment evinced by the "Camelot" letter without understanding just how thoroughly Rogers is committed to speaking the language of the day. This disease of contemporaneity seems to affect his associates as well. Ten years after the letter incident, Howard Kirschenbaum, Rogers's biographer, could write: "I have read some ten thousand or more pages of Rogers's published and unpublished writings; yet 'Camelot—A Fable Retold' moves me most of all."

Rogers's other reply to his critics is that they simply haven't discovered what he has discovered, through his clients, about human nature. Deep instincts, once you get in contact with them, are good and trustworthy. At the core, the human being is basically constructive, socialized, and creatively healthy. His main argument on this point is derived from an analogy with the animal world: "If I endeavored to explain to you that if the 'lion-ness' of the lion were to be released, or the 'sheep-ness' of the sheep, that these animals would then be impelled by insatiable lusts, uncontrollable aggressions, wild and excessive sexual behaviors, and tendencies of innate destructiveness, you would quite properly laugh at me. Obviously, such a view is pure nonsense." This conviction that the natural way—i.e., the spontaneous, unsolicited way—is best is the basis for Rogers's belief that it is safe to let each person follow his own truth. Evil does not exist; at least it does not exist in persons who are in touch with themselves. Those in a state of nature will naturally act in mutually enhancing ways; each can pursue his desires without infringing on others.

It is Rogers's belief, in short, that the Fall never happened, and that Eden is just around the corner or, more accurately, within. Essentially the humanistic movement in psychology is an attempt to recover the paradisaical state where sex is free and innocent, where no judgments are made, and where guilt does not exist. The most characteristic element in Rogers's thought is a remarkable—one is tempted to say incredible—faith in human nature. The deep inner self—the true self—can always be counted on. It is well-nigh infallible, a sort of supreme Pontiff within. Rogers stands as a classic example of the fact that a religious temperament is not easily discarded. His descriptions of human possibilities and human potentials have the same reverential tone that a believer uses when speaking of God. The awe in this case is not awe of God, but of the healthy self-regulation of the human organism. All of which may go to show that you can take the psychologist out of the seminary, but you can't take the seminarian out of the psychologist.

* * *

Two years after the small seminar, Rogers is back in the Boston area as one of six leaders of a weekend "person-centered" workshop on "releasing individual and community power." Some of the issues which were present in embryonic form at the seminar are now become full-grown—problems of midlife, loneliness, suffering, aging, and death. Moreover, the somewhat submerged spiritual concerns of the earlier meeting have now bubbed to the surface.

This time one hundred and ten people are gathered in a large carpeted room; most are sitting on the floor conversing in small clusters. The workshop has no official point of departure. After about an hour of small-talk one gentleman (not one of the leaders) raises his voice: "I just wanted to say that I'm just happy to be here." That's all he says. The room lapses into awkward silence. After a minute another person says, "I just wanted to thank you all for making me feel comfortable in this large group. I just know that this is going to be a beautiful experience." Another silence.

"I'm more used to TORRE," says a white-haired, bearded man.

"What's TORRE?"

"TORRE means Trusting, Open, Real Relationship Experience. It's a group on Long Island. I like to think of it as being like a yogurt culture because it's always spreading."

"What *is* the TORRE?"

"The TORRE can't be defined because I create the Torre for me. If that sounds mysterious, it is mysterious"

"No, it sounds exciting."

"Fantastic."

Judy, a thirtyish blonde, retorts, "I haven't had TORRE, but I've had a hell of a lot of personal power!"

Another woman suggests, "I would love to see the room in a different way. I wonder if there's another way to change this room so that I would feel more comfortable?"

"I'm enjoying the warmth and closeness in this room," says another young woman. "I feel warm and close to everyone in the room. I think it's amazing that there are so many people in here with so little structure."

The "discussion" continues in this vein. "Sometimes," observes a young man, "I'm walking down the street feeling and seeing others' presence, but I can't make contact. I came here to learn how to give strokes and get them."

A young bearded man: "I feel energized. I don't have to play games—just be myself. If I choose to talk that's OK, and if I choose not to, that's OK too. I have the feeling that there are lots of brothers and sisters and cousins here."

A woman with an English accent: "I feel comfortable already."

A wiry-haired woman: "I don't experience any of this!"

Carl Rogers: "Thank you for saying this."

The young bearded man who feels energized (his name is Barry) reassures her, "It will happen. It's happening already."

"I want to share with you . . ."

"I want to thank you for sharing with me."

"I hear you."

"I hear two things in that."

"Could you tell me what you need?"

"I want to share how I feel about what you said you felt about what I said."

"I can relate to what you say. . . ."

In all of his work, Rogers stresses the importance of process over content. The self is a process, and one should not try to define it; learning is a process; communication is a process. In *Freedom to Learn* he writes: "The most socially useful learning in the world is the learning of the process of learning, a continuous openness to experience and incorporation into oneself of the process of change. . . . change is the central fact of life." The idea of an education from Rogers's perspective is not to learn history or literature or physics—because these things are always changing—but to develop process skills. Ditto for values clarification courses: you don't learn particular values, you learn "the valuing process."

One irony of this elevation of process over content is that, put into practice, it often results in something quite the opposite of the freshness and spontaneity it is meant to secure. It is one thing to have communications skills, and another thing to have something to communicate. Imagine a man who has taken ten courses in communication skills, but has never had a course in history or literature or science, and who further has no interest in business, sports, religion, or current politics. His only interest is in communicating. He will be very good at expressions of understanding and empathy, he will be a good listener, as they say, but finally there will be something lacking to his conversation. When there is nothing to communicate except communications skills, conversation becomes banal and predictable. Putting together a roomful of such people results in a great deal of process, but precious little progress. It is interesting to note in this connection that Kurt Back's thorough and excellent analysis of encounter groups is titled simply *Beyond Words*. Mr. Back was not implying that there is something ineffable about encounter groups. In the end, he suggests, there is nothing to convey. People are forced to hug one another to make up for the emptiness of the language.

A good deal of hugging is taking place already in the

group, despite the fact that most of the people here did not know each other before today. Kurt Back observed that members of encounter groups tend to use each other as tools to get a strong emotional experience: "What people within the group forget is simply that it would not have mattered who was in the group at all, that people are completely interchangeable. The particular personality of the other people is not relevant; there is nothing personal in the relationship. . . ." Once again it is process and not content that counts. It's important to have relationship skills, to be able to engage in the relationship process, but the actual object of your affections doesn't seem to count as much.

Given the fluid nature of the healthy person a la Rogers, lasting relationships—the kind that would depend on the character or content rather than the skills of the couple—come to seem untenable—unless (happy coincidence) two people might grow and flow in the same direction, or unless they are willing to give each other a great deal of "space." Rogers, in any event, seems quite reconciled to short-term relationships. In his graduation address to students at Sonoma State College (the commencement where the medieval trappings were discarded) Rogers advised that:

> The man of the future . . . will be living his transient life mostly in temporary relationships. . . . he must be able to establish closeness quickly. He must be able to leave these close relationships behind without excessive conflict or mourning.

A statement like this raises the question of how close a relationship can be that is gotten in and out of with so little cost. But one would be mistaken to think that close relationships have the highest place in Rogers's pantheon. Qualities such as self-actualization and change rank much higher. It would be difficult to overestimate the importance he puts on change. A careful reading of Rogers suggests that he would much rather see people in process than in a close relationship. "Life, at its best, is a flowing, changing process in which nothing is fixed," wrote Rogers in 1961. This, it may be noted, is not the best we can expect out of an unpredictable life: this is "life at its best."

Rogers's biography reveals a man in love with the idea of motion. Upon leaving the University of Chicago to begin work at the University of Wisconsin, he wrote a letter of explanation to the Counseling Center staff. The last part of it is worth quoting at length:

> I tried once to tell staff in a memo—you may remember it— what a large streak of pioneering spirit there is in me. I really am kin to the old frontiersman, and my feeling at the present time is that I can hardly wait to throw my pack on my back and leave the settlement behind. I itch to get going! . . . The thought of new wilderness to explore . . . is like wine in my blood. . . .
>
> So if what I am saying in this memo seems to you as if I am talking to you from a distance, halfway up the ridge on the trail of a new adventure, you are right, for that is the way it is. What I hope you will realize is that this in no way alters my affection for you, but is simply my need to keep going.

This revealing letter captures the mood and purpose of much present-day psychology: the spirit of individualism, the impatience with settled ways, the need to keep growing and changing. Humanistic psychology represents the spirit of the frontier applied to the self. If there are no more open areas to move to, then the self itself must be opened up. Moreover, it reveals how much Rogers is in the American mainstream. In Rogers one hears echos not only of the pioneers and mountain men, but of earlier explorers of the inner self such as Emerson, Thoreau, and Whitman. Whitman, for example, considered himself to be a "cosmos," while Thoreau talked about exploring "the Atlantic and Pacific Ocean of one's being alone." Like modern-day human potentialists, they all had difficulties with

163

striking a balance between complete self-containment and complete merging of selves, sounding like rugged individualists one moment, pantheists the next. But it seems safe to say that, like Rogers, their interests tended toward the self-in-process rather than the self-in-relationship.

The process is obviously the thing that matters here in the workshop. Despite the advertised purpose—"On Releasing Personal and Community Power"—it soon becomes evident that no techniques or procedures for doing so will be forthcoming. Like the earlier seminar, the workshop has no set content. There is no real work for the group except the expression of feeling.

Along with the contentless pleasantries, however, there quickly develops within the group an equally contentless hostility. One of the most common openers is, "I'm very angry!" "I'm very angry. Why are you trying to lay your trip on him?" or "I'm very angry at you. You're not giving me space to be myself!" or "What you say makes me very angry—not as a man, which isn't important, but as a person!"

Up to this point, the main problem of the workshop has been the question of whether to stay in one large group or to break up into smaller groups. On the one hand, the group is obviously too big to function in any coherent manner. It would make sense to divide up. On the other hand, there could be no worse fate than being stuck in an uninteresting group. The main objection to smaller groups seems to be the fear of missing something. It is the question of whether to have a three-ring circus or a one-ring circus. The important thing is to crowd as much raw experience into the day as possible without being left out of the real action. And there is a conviction, implicit but apparent, that not much action has occurred. During all this time, for example, Dr. Rogers has said nothing except to the handful of people directly around him. The other five leaders also have made no attempt to lead.

Finally, after fully eight hours of unorganized gropings, the real action comes. Debbie, a petite woman in her early twenties, stands up, her face contorted: "I'm damned angry at all of you!" she shouts. "I have needs, and my needs are important to me, and my needs aren't being met in this group. This group is too big to give me the support I need. And I have a right to have my needs met! I'm leaving right now! I'm going into the other room, and if anyone wants to come with me they can, and if they don't that's their business!"

As she makes to leave, Curtis, one of the leaders, shouts, "How about my needs, Debbie? How about my needs to be heard by you in a large group? My needs are important too!"

Debbie starts walking. But before she can go two steps a large middle-aged woman in a shapeless print dress grabs her by the wrists. "Debbie, don't go! Don't go! I need you here!" she pleads.

Debbie breaks the hold and keeps on walking. The woman reaches out to the air in a gesture of desperation and cries out hysterically, "Debbie, you're rejecting me! You're rejecting me! Debbie, I need you here!" (Debbie keeps walking; she's almost to the door.) "My God! She's rejecting me! I have needs too! What about my needs?" (Debbie disappears through the door.) "My God! Please help me! Please help me! I need help! I'm so alone! I need your support! Please! Please!"

Certain members of the group move over to the woman and start hugging her. About twenty other people drift into the other room, following Debbie's lead.

What does one do when needs collide? It is a problem not only for this group, but for human potentialists in general. What makes it problematic is that the humble everyday solution of subordinating your needs to someone else's is a thought that simply does not occur. If Rogers is correct, such a resolution is unnecessary. He says that our needs can be gratified without pain to others, that we can safely move away from pleasing others because there are natural balancing forces within each person which act to make self-interest coincide with the interest of the group (*On Becoming a Person*, Chapters 8 and 9). This, as sociologist Thomas Kreilkamp points out (in *The Corrosion of the Self*), is a psychological version of Adam Smith's economics. Kreilkamp notes accurately that Rogers does truly believe in respecting and regarding other people and their needs. The trouble is that he makes no provision for those cases where the duty that I owe myself runs into the needs of others. That there might be a point at which, even among the most aware of the aware, group needs contradict individual needs, a point at which one or the other has to give in, is a point that Rogers seems unwilling to concede.

If that seems stubborn, it is worth considering that it is really no more stubborn than Thoreau, Emerson, or Whitman— or Adam Smith—were being in expressing similar points of view. Here again Rogers is simply expressing his quintessential Americanism—that is, the Americanism of "Self-Reliance" and *Walden* and "The Song of Myself," or the Americanism of Huck Finn on the raft. Rogers belongs to that tradition of American thinkers who are engaged in what Quentin Anderson calls "the flight from culture." "I must be myself," wrote Emerson, "I cannot break myself any longer for you or you." Culture, family, community, tradition represent for Rogers, as they did for Emerson, almost unbearable impositions on the free development of the individual.

In today's session, the free development of the individual has led Debbie off into the other room where she can find both more space and more support. Meanwhile Lilliane, the woman who had pleaded for her to stay, is pouring out her troubles to a new set of listeners. Her problem, it turns out, is that her daughters are going off to college, leaving her with a husband she can't count on for emotional support.

Suddenly another outburst of crying erupts in the small circle that has formed around Lilliane. Carol, a woman in her midtwenties, begins to sob, "I wish I had a mother to love me! I never had a mother to love me!" Lilliane hugs her, and a man says, "We love you." Another ventures, "I'm here for you, and I'm really feeling the pain you're going through." "You can lean on me," says another.

"We love you." The radical egalitarianism of Rogerian psychology suggests that not only are all people equal, but so are all relationships. Blood relationships aren't any better than any other kind, and maybe worse judging by the way they confine and warp us. Animals, who are more in tune with natural processes, learn to break free of their parents rather quickly. It all goes back to the idea that the relating *process*, not the particular relationship, is what counts. Considering this, it is not surprising to find human potential types in the forefront of efforts to redefine relationships so that a family, for instance, may include anybody who lives together in any manner. They have, in addition, been active in seeking to establish all sorts of "support communities" that don't rely on blood ties. There is nothing particularly special about a mother-child relationship. It's quality that counts, not kind. If you didn't get love from your mother, that's OK now because "We love you" and "I'm here for you" and "You can count on me."

But no one seems able to hold center stage for very long. The process of change won't allow for it. The discussion now shifts back to the secession. Did the small group have the right to leave the big group? Opinion is divided. Although the general agreement is that people have a right to their own space, there is a feeling that the "community," as it is now being called, has an almost sacred character, and to break it up is a kind of schism. Carl Rogers has the last word on the subject. "You know," he says, "this is exactly what happens in a one-to-one relationship when one of the partners feels the need for freedom . . . and I guess if we're going to respect that individual as a person, we've got to give them that space."

The next day and the next the theme of anger still predominates. Some of it seems unfocused, and even manufactured for the ocasion. Christopher Lasch maintains that the narcissistic person is locked in a permanent, primitive rage. But one doesn't have to look that deep for an explanation. After awhile it becomes clear that one of the best ways to gain attention in this large assembly (by now the secessionists have returned) is to shout out your anger—the louder and angrier, the better. It is past the point where a heart-felt "I'm feeling really energized" will merit much notice. In this context, the notion of getting in touch with the wisdom of the child-within dawns with a new meaning. Sometimes, as every wise child knows, the only way to get attention is to throw a tantrum.

The best combination, however, is anger tinged with anguish. Rita, a woman in her midthirties, begins to sob and shout. She is in "incredible pain." She relates the story of a relationship gone on the rocks. Now she can never trust a man again. She's not really sure she can trust any of us. She's not sure our emotions are real enough. But she chances it. Her relationship? She made it plain from the start, she tells us, that it must be on her terms. She is a successful businesswoman, a "very strong person" in a "high-powered job" who jets from power center to power center. *He* had to accept that she could only be around a few days out of the month. In addition, he had to prove himself by leaving his wife and children and moving to California. He's done all this, but now, it seems, he wants her to change in some way (it is difficult to tell what with the sobbing). She's opened herself up to him, allowed herself to fall in love, and now he wants her to change. Well, she can't do that. She's got to be herself. Besides, she can now see that she fell in love with the wrong man. It's obvious that by the time he's forty he'll be stuck in a back office somewhere. She needs a high-powered, strong, successful person like herself.

Another woman, Carol, has been hugging Rita through all this. Now Carol complains of a similar problem. Somehow the more independent she becomes, the more separated she becomes from others. Dr. Rogers offers some sympathetic clarification: "You feel, 'damn it, the more free I get, the more lonesome I become!' " Carol actually had used stronger language than this, but Rogers seems to have an aversion toward vulgarities. One gets the impression, though, that he is really feeling her frustration.

These revelations bring a chorus of like complaints from other women. A good-looking blonde woman with a gold cross about her neck relates that she also was fooled by a man. She thought he admired her strength, but he really envied her success. In the end he just couldn't keep up with the competition. A middle-aged black woman joins in to tell how she outgrew her first husband who "couldn't keep up with my changes." These men, she says, are all looking for mothers. Much approval—at least from the female ranks—greets this remark.

Finally a young bearded man puts in a defense of the male branch of persons. They really aren't such bad sorts, and besides, he himself can't find a woman to trust though he's tried and tried—and he's "given them space."

These are ill-chosen words.

Little Debbie shouts him down: "YOU GIVE! YOU GIVE! YOU CAN'T GIVE A FEMALE ANYTHING! PEOPLE CAN'T MAKE GIFTS OF SPACE TO OTHERS. YOU'VE GOT TO TAKE YOUR OWN SPACE! NOBODY GIVES IT TO YOU!"

Her own husband, who sits close by, looks and acts like a Caspar Milquetoast. One gets the impression that he is tolerated precisely because he doesn't take up much space.

After Debbie's tirade, a moment of silence ensues—enough for Bernice's quiet crying to be heard. Bernice had been the hostess at the earlier seminar; it was she who introduced Dr. Rogers with a moment of meditation. She has lost another man, and she doesn't know why. She's lost something deep inside, and doesn't know if she'll ever get it back. It's the same thing that was lost two years ago. In fact, she uses almost exactly the same words as she had then. But it seems that much more of "it" is gone now. She feels all alone and withdrawn.

In reply to Bernice, a neatly dressed, kindly woman of about fifty-five offers some words of consolation and advice. What she has learned from her own experience is this: "Sometimes you've got to lose yourself before you can find yourself." The plain, heavy wooden cross hung from her neck suggests that she might be a nun. Roman Catholic nuns quite regularly participate in groups of this sort. "You've got to lose yourself before you find yourself." Perhaps so. But what sense does such advice make except within a religious context? Apparently this woman is in contact with a tradition that stands outside human potentialism—a tradition that may have something to offer besides clarification of feelings. And now it comes back to her. But the advice doesn't seem to register here. It is wildly out of context. Human potentialism may be a religion of sorts, but it is not a religion of dying to self.

The focus of attention is now shifting rapidly from one claimant to another. The workshop is nearing its close. Carmel, a woman in her late twenties, makes her final bid for attention. She has already had a disproportionate amount of it. Over the last three days she has been an avid practitioner of Debbie's dictum, "You've got to take your own space." It's plain she's been working herself up for this. She is literally jumping up and down, trying to catch the group's notice, and for the last five minutes she has been making sporadic exclamations such as "My God!" or "This is awful!" She obviously has run out of things to talk about, but with the meeting coming to a close and her needs still unmet, there is no time to worry about fine points. Finally, like a shopper elbowing her way to the bargain table, she simply pushes in: "This is awful! I have needs! I'm having trouble too!"

She is having trouble with Barry (who sits beside her); she's not sure their relationship can last much longer. She's not sure that anything lasts, or that she can count on these other people. She feels she hasn't received enough time and working through here, and *dammit,* she deserves it.

Once again another older woman tries to bring a sense of proportion to the proceedings. Many of those present, she says gently but firmly, weren't able to get attention, but that is just in the nature of large groups. And she reminds Carmel of all the attention and support she had received earlier in the day.

"That's the way my mother talks!" Carmel shouts, "and I don't want to listen to it! Don't give me this count-your-blessings bull! I deserve support. I need people to give to me!"

It must be noted that Rogers has several times stated in his books and articles that simple awareness of feelings is often enough. Feelings need not always be expressed. This point seems to have eluded Carmel. In other respects, however, her treatment of the older woman is well within Rogerian boundaries. Age merits no special consideration in an age of change. Unless an older person keeps up with change, she has no more to offer than anyone else. "I feel a great pity," wrote Rogers in 1974, "for those persons I know who are growing into old age without the continuing stimulation of younger minds and younger life styles. Certainly for the last thirty-five years any real learning (for me) from professional sources have come from those who were younger."

In that same article he again takes up the theme of the "emerging person." "Emerging through the ruins is the new person, highly aware, self-directing, an explorer of inner space perhaps more than outer space, scornful of the conformity of institutions and the dogma of authority." Rogers has been heralding the emerging person for quite some time, so it seems not unfair to ask, Where is he? Is he here in this group? Is Carmel the emerging person? Is Carol? Is Debbie or Barry or Bernice or Rita? One sees some of the futuristic person here: the scorn of tradition, of anything passed down from generation to generation, of the wisdom of the ages or the aged, of appeals to any

171

authority outside oneself. Still, the promise of emergent whole-ness and harmony seems strangely elusive—unless the expression of unbridled emotion is what makes us most ourselves.

T. S. Eliot suggested that it does not. In an essay on Thomas Hardy he wrote:

> But it is by no means self-evident that human beings are most real when most violently excited; violent physical passions do not in themselves differentiate men from each other but rather tend to reduce them to the same state; and the passion has significance only in relation to the character and behavior of the man at other moments of his life and in other contexts. Furthermore, a strong passion is only inter-esting or significant in strong men; those who abandon themselves without resistance to excitements which tend to deprive them of reason, become merely instruments of feeling and lose their humanity.

What makes men most real—that is, strong enough to lend significance to their emotions? In the view taken by Eliot, what makes us most real is not our natural self but our cultural self. Ironically, the primitives, that is, real primitives, line up on the side of Eliot, not Rogers or Rousseau. No savage believes in the myth of the "noble savage." Given the opportunity, primitive peoples tend to dispose their lives ceremoniously rather than naturally. Restraint, gesture, deference, and ritual make the man, not Nature. Like Eliot, they may be considered elitists. If one can take the word of an expert like Mircea Eliade, the primitive man hates and fears sameness or homogeneity most of all. The lack of differentiation that characterizes the Rogerian product is precisely what they wish to avoid, for it represents a return to the primal chaos from which they have been delivered. Primal chaos is the state of complete egalitarianism that existed before creation, when everything was equal to everything else and all was equal to nothing. Nothing special existed; nothing was deserving of special attention. Out of this smothering lava, God or gods created order: an ordered, hierarchical universe in which everything was given a place and a name and a meaning. It is fear of the primal homogeniety and the wish for something more which sets primitive man to chanting and making sacrifice and erecting totems. Primitive man seeks hierarchy and transcendence. He wishes to be connected with the sacred realm, which means the ordered realm. Men are most real when they imitate the Gods. So men who are truly interested in preserving the uniqueness of man see to it that special times and places are set aside where a man can be most himself: sacred groves and temples, sacred feasts and seasons, and anointed priests to preside over them. Men seek hierarchy because hierarchy is a way to rise out of the natural self and become the real self.

Of course, this conception of life is not the exclusive property of primitives. It has until recently been the ordering motif of Western civilization. Men are thought to be unique, but their uniqueness is to be found in taking their place in an ordered society. Man is a work of art, but a work of art needs the ordering backdrop of a museum or gallery to make manifest its specialness. A painting carelessly jumbled on a cellar floor with other paintings is just another picture. In this view, place is just as important as personality; personal identity is thought to be wrapped up in some way with one's position or role. Peeling away roles is like peeling an onion. When all the layers are gone, we are left with a surprisingly small kernel. Strip the self of its roles and relationships, says the voice of tradition, and what you have is not some immeasurable cosmos within, but a skinny, shivering fellow looking rather foolish in his nakedness.

It is in this context that traditional rules of conduct, manner, and deference acquire their meaning. Though one may disagree with an elder, one still accedes place to him because place is extremely important for all of us. Without it, we all sink back into that primitive morass where one place is as good as another, where quality is drowned in equality. This attitude accounts for the fact that the ancients were much concerned over placing themselves not only within a lineage and a tradition, but also within a physical locale. Odysseus, for instance, was always at pains to announce himself as "Odysseus, Laertes' son of Ithaca." Of such elements are identies made. Even today, and even among psychologists—though not psychologists of the Rogerian school—the importance of place to identity is recognized. Erik Erikson's theories about identity are a case in point. Though Erikson's concept of identity is sometimes misconstrued to be about the establishment of independence, it does in fact have much more to do with place, context, history, tradition, and generational continuity. Identity confusion stems precisely from an inability to fit in or find a place for ourselves.

One way to appreciate the concern with place, both ancient and modern, is to have the experience of attending a conference in a large city, as I did recently in Chicago. Many of these conferences are now held in hotels at or beside the airport, which means that unless you take special pains you are unlikely to see the city itself. Because airport areas and the hotels which serve them are practically indistinguishable from one another, you are left with the strange feeling of being nowhere in particular. You could be in Chicago or Los Angeles or Houston or Baltimore. You may be left with the slightly guilty feeling that I had of not having traveled at all. "How was Chicago?" the folks back home will ask. A perfectly honest answer might be: "Like nothing in particular." This, of course, is only a faint hint of homogeniety, not quite the undifferentiated chaos of primal times, but it does seem a step in that direction.

The participants in the workshop are truly new-age people who probably do not concern themselves whether they are in Chicago or Houston. "Here we are in this situation," they seem to be saying; "the rest of our lives isn't relevant. We can be real and caring to each other right here and right now."

There is no question of sincerity here. This is the way they feel. Something, however, seems lacking in the quality of their love and acceptance. It has that nothing-in-particular feel about it, as though anyone could be substituted for anyone else, and the process of caring would just keep rolling along. The things that normally give significance to emotions—family, history, roles, religion—have been stripped away here. As a result, the lack of character, the interchangeableness, the leveling that Kurt Back noticed in his study of encounter groups characterizes this group as well.

A remark of George Steiner seems apropos. During a television interview with Bill Moyers, Moyers, having misinterpreted Steiner's previous remark, asked, "Does that mean, 'To thine own self be true?' " Replied Steiner, "I'm afraid that's pretty small beer in most cases." The self—pretty small beer? Steiner could never get away with saying that in this group. At the least he would be pitied for his poor self-concept. More likely he would be yelled at for "putting down" the group. For there seems to be an unspoken but mutual conspiracy here that once the stripping away has been accomplished, everyone must then switch to the role of a Columbus, awestruck at having discovered a new world. The self after all is the center of the humanistic faith. If it should turn out to be a false god, there would be nothing left. So the ceremonials that attend the discovery of self have a distinctly religious tone, and certain thoughts, such as the idea that the self is overrated, are unthinkable.

When the self takes on the status of a god, it is inevitable that sooner or later it must have immortality conferred on it. On the third day of the workshop, in the morning session, just such an apotheosis occurs. At first there is no hint that today will be any different from yesterday. Barry starts it off by saying, "I want to thank you all for what happened yesterday because I really feel real now because of what happened. You allowed me to be myself, and that's great." This brings a familiar litany of "That's beautiful" and similiar sentiments, and induces one man to say, "I want to thank me for allowing myself to be myself" (applause).

175

But before the sense of deja vu is ten minutes old something novel happens. The day before, Dr. Rogers had mentioned his wife Helen's recent death, and now Lynn wants to tell him how deeply she felt on hearing it. At this Rogers begins to sob. Several group members rush over, hug him, and kneel at his feet. Through his sobs he tells the story of his relationship with his wife: their long happy marriage, the unhappiness of the last five years, her illness, her strange dreams of devils, her bitterness over other women who were no more than friends of his, his decision to lead his own life separate from Helen. During this recounting, small tableaus of crying people begin to form across the room. In one group the crying is particularly audible. When Rogers pauses ten minutes later, a young woman from this group tearfully tells of her brother's death and how she missed her opportunity to say good-bye. Now it's too late.

Or is it? A number of group members crowd around her, and one young man assures her that it's not too late: "Do you want to say good-bye to him right now? Say it now." She has clammed up now, however; this is perhaps more than she was prepared for. Rogers offers his personal encouragement: "Three years ago I would have thought this was stupid, but now I would say that he *can* hear you." These last words are spoken slowly and with emphasis. Rogers continues: "I never used to believe in immortality, but now all the evidence shows that there's something to it. I used to believe that death was the end, but now it seems that there is another side." Has Rogers given second thoughts to his discarded Christianity? No. This is an experientially based learning. Rogers discovered the "other side" three years ago in the company of Helen and a medium in Brazil. At the seance Helen Rogers had made contact with her dead sister, tables moved, voices were heard, names were spelled out, the table hit Helen in the stomach. It was extraordinary to say the least. Rogers is convinced now that there is another world, and that it is possible to contact those on the other side of the veil.

He is all the more convinced because he has been in contact with Helen. It came about this way: At the time of Helen's death, he had coincidentally formed a new relationship, but the juxtaposition of the two events had left him with a powerful sense of guilt. He knows rationally that he shouldn't have felt guilty, but he did. He was miserable with guilt. Then the strange thing happened. One day he was consulting a Ouija board—now he never believed in Ouija boards before, mind you, and he knows this will sound strange—and suddenly letters began to form (or he heard a voice—this part is not clear). It is Helen, and her message is one of complete absolution: "Enjoy, Carl, enjoy! Be free! Be free!"

"Well by gosh!" says Rogers, and he wipes his hand upward across his brow. "What a wave of relief swept over me when I heard that."

From the group, exclamations of awe can be heard: "That's incredible!" "Fantastic!" And now it seems everyone in the group has had their mystical and quasi-mystical experiences: coincidences surrounding death, premonitional dreams, poltergeists, and encounters with something known as "the white light." Whenever the latter is mentioned there are nods of familiarity, as though the white light were an old friend or a new G.E. product.

Rogers's growing spiritual interest is recorded in his most recent book *A Way of Being*. Here he adds a few more details about Helen's closing days, how she "had visions of an inspiring white light which came close, lifted her from the bed, and then deposited her back on the bed," and how on the evening of her death friends made contact with Helen through a medium and learned how she had experienced spirits coming for her, and how she now had the form of a young woman.

"I now consider it possible," he writes, "that each of us is a continuing spiritual essence lasting over time, and occasionally incarnated in a human body."

This is followed by a chapter entitled "Do We Need a

Reality?" The gist of the chapter is that, no, we do not. The universe is best thought of as a "great *thought*" rather than a reality. There are as many realities as there are people. And what is real for me now is not real for me tomorrow. For support of his thesis he musters together such luminaries as Carl Jung, John Lily (of talking dolphin and sensory awareness fame), and Carlos Castaneda. Lily, for example, like other mystics before him, "experienced the universe as a unity, a unity based on love." The upshot of what we are now seeing is "that a vast and mysterious universe—perhaps an inner reality, or perhaps a spirit world of which we are all unknowingly a part—seems to exist." Rogers concludes this latest opus by taking up once again the theme of the emerging person. This time, however, the emerging person has picked up a new quality—"a yearning for the spiritual."

While all this hankering after the spirit world may seem more in keeping with the religion of Mary Baker Eddy than with the psychological profession, Rogers can hardly be called out of place. The truth is that psychologists have never been able to keep their nose out of religion. Carl Jung's work was nothing less than an attempt to create a new religion, and even Freud, who dismissed Jung as a "messiah," was unable to refrain from writing about *Moses* and *Monotheism* or *The Future of an Illusion*. Wilhelm Reich was mainly interested in "Cosmic Life Energy" and considered himself to be in the same league as Jesus Christ. William James not only wrote about religious experiences, but had some of his own—very Jungian and mystical experiences. During his later years, Abraham Maslow concentrated more and more on topics such as "transcendence," "mystical fusion," and "high Nirvana"; he also wrote a book on religious experience. Not to be outdone by his colleagues in the profession, Erich Fromm quoted copiously from the writings of Buddha and from the Old Testament, though mostly from Buddha. Fromm wrote a book titled *You Shall Be as Gods*—and he meant it. Elizabeth Kubler-Ross, the psychiatrist whose work created for psychology the brand new field of thanatology, has also, like Rogers, become interested, indeed mainly interested, in contacting those who have gone beyond. Mention should also be made of the International Association of Transpersonal Psychologists, who claim to be the fastest-growing branch of psychology and who specialize in ESP, paranormal phenomena, reincarnation, and out-of-body experiences.

The list goes on and on. What is noteworthy about it is that almost to a man the type of religion they are plumping for is some form or other of Eastern religion or at best (as in the case of Jung) a vague kind of gnosticism. Most Eastern religions are, of course, forms of pantheism. And pantheism, paradoxically, is a particular temptation to individualistic democracies like America, since it tends to relieve somewhat the chief burden of such societies—the burden of being an individual. Pantheism, so to speak, lets you melt into the crowd. Tocqueville, who had noted accurately that Americans had more of a passion for equality than for liberty, also observed that pantheism was the philosophy "most fitted to seduce the human mind" in a democracy.

The other dominant strand in Eastern thinking is mind over matter. Hinduism maintains that all matter is illusory, while Buddhism asserts that even spiritual "realities" are illusions. Mind is the only thing. A good mind, one that is in touch with the Universal Mind, can think realities into existence, and can think them right out of existence too. Mary Baker Eddy believed this. And today a growing number of psychologists of the humanistic and transpersonal schools are arriving at the same conclusion. What this works out to in the American mind is a powerful belief in the power of positive thinking: the idea that thinking makes it so. Emerson and Thoreau were imbued with the notion; so was William James. Carl Rogers believes in it too. "Do we need a reality?" Not if it gets in our way. "Let each person create his own reality"—that seems to be the credo imbedded in Rogers's latest cogitations.

Some humanistic psychologists have already gone far beyond Rogers in this matter. Will Schutz, the author of *Joy* and

179

Profound Simplicity, argues that we don't have to die if we don't choose to, and that airplanes we fly in won't crash if we don't want them to. But it is Rogers's endorsement that gives the whole enterprise—the eastward movement—the respectability it needs to really take hold. Whether Eastern mysticism is the final destination of humanistic psychology remains to be seen, but it's worth remembering how many times Rogers has been on the cutting edge of psychological and cultural change.

The seemingly bizarre erruption of spirituality during the workshop turns out to be, then, not an aberration, but the logical working out of themes long present in American psychology and American democracy. The real problem in this working-out process does not lie in accepting some form of spirituality. That part is surprisingly easy. The difficulty lies in reconciling the search for transcendence with the search for equality. Like any other humans in any other society, we want something more than the humdrum of daily existence. We want to live intensely, and above all we want to be in touch with the cosmic forces. We seem to need a religion. And since psychology is in the business of fulfilling needs, it has given us a religion. If it is not yet a full-grown religion, it is certainly in the process of slouching toward LaJolla to be born.

From the primitive and elitist points of view, of course, we are going about it in the wrong way. Too much stress on equality makes transcendence impossible. Locating the cosmic forces within us means that there is no escape. And besides, they might argue, how can you have a religion without authority, hierarchy, and respect for elders? Finally, they might wonder, "What is the point of self-acceptance without prior transformation of the self?" To just accept the self as it is, unredeemed, uninitiated, undisciplined by bonds of loyalty and oath, is the antithesis of transcendence. In any event, pantheism would be a poor place to begin, since it represents a temptation to give up the quest for hierarchy and transcendence right at the start and just settle for sinking your soul into the next fellow's. That would constitute a dangerous courting of primal chaos.

It is sometimes hard to avoid the impression that Rogers *is* courting chaos. In his writings he keeps referring to our society as a "disintegrating culture," and he seems pleased with the thought. When he writes, "The conception of a real world, obvious to anyone, is rapidly slipping completely out of my grasp," there is no hint of panic in it. As his psychology travels eastward, so does his epistemology. What we call "matter," what we think of as reality, is what the Hindus call *maya*—illusion. Rogers has bought into the philosophy, just as Mary Baker Eddy did years ago. This helps to explain his curious treatment of pain and suffering. It is not true, as some of Rogers's critics maintain, that he never talks about affliction. Rogers writes often enough about bitterness, sorrow, loss, and anxiety; but he manages to talk about them in such a way that they seem no longer to carry any sting. The mood he creates can be felt in the following interchange between he and a client who has confessed to feelings of murderous rage:

> C: And then of course, I've come to—to see and to feel that over this—see, I've covered it up. *(Weeps.)* But I've covered it up with so much bitterness, which in turn I had to cover up. *(Weeping) That's* what I want to get rid of! I almost don't care if I hurt.

> T: *(Softly, and with an empathic tenderness toward the hurt she is experiencing)* You feel that here at the basis of it as you experience it is a feeling of real tears for yourself. But that you can't show, mustn't show, so that's been covered by bitterness that you don't like, that you'd like to be rid of. You almost feel you'd rather absorb the hurt than to—than to feel the bitterness. *(Pause)* And what you seem to be saying quite strongly is, I do *hurt,* and I've tried to cover it up.

C: I didn't *know* it.

T: M-hm. Like a new discovery really.
(from On Becoming a Person)

Pain is an experience. To learn to get in touch with your experience, to learn to flow with your experience is like—well, it's "Like a new discovery really." Whatever they may feel about their suffering outside the counseling situation, Rogers's clients do seem to get on friendlier terms with their distress within the climate he creates. "It's an adventure," says one, "that's what it is—into the unknown. . . . I'm beginning to enjoy this now, I'm joyful about it, even about all these old negative things." There is something of the Christian mystic in the mood Rogers creates in people: suffering viewed as a mysterious mingling of pain and ecstacy. The trick is that Rogers seems to get people to accept it for the sole sake of feeling the flow of experience in them, while the benighted saints put up with it for the sake of God. At bottom it's not a Christian attitude at all, but an Eastern one: sit back and watch the Magic Theatre—the illusory flow of experience. Pain is no different from pleasure, pleasure no different from pain. All is one. Once you create this mood, any subject may be broached without disturbance. It seems to be the mood of the country. Talk about death, for instance, with any group of college-educated people and they invariably say things like, "I look upon death as a part of life" or "I think of death as a learning experience."

Positive thinking. That is the secret of the East. Mind over matter. The veil of illusion pierced. Death? Pain? Does any of it really exist? Does anything exist? Rogers claims to be in the existential tradition, but the tone is all wrong for an existentialist. When Kierkegaard wrote about fear and trembling and the sickness unto death, when Pascal encountered the abyss, or when Sartre spoke of nausea, they were genuinely afraid. Rogers meets all these things head-on with the placid equanimity of a smiling Buddha. Evidently some people like the encounter with Nothingness. William Barrett suggests that indeed this is true:

> The Chinese Taoists found the Great Void tranquilizing, peaceful, even joyful. For the Buddists in India, the idea of Nothing evoked a mood of universal compassion for all creatures caught in the toils of an existence that is ultimately groundless. In the traditional culture of Japan the idea of Nothingness pervades the exquisite modes of aesthetic feeling displayed in painting, architecture, and even the ceremonial rituals of daily life. But Western man, up to his neck in *things,* objects, and the business of mastering them, recoils with anxiety from any possible encounter with Nothingness and labels talk of it negative—which is to say, morally reprehensible.

Poor Western man. Rogers's hope, expressed in his latest book, is that he may serve as a bridge between Eastern thought and Western thought. But judging from *A Way of Being,* the bridge may be designed for one-way traffic only.

Kurt Back observed that the weakness of the encounter session does not become apparent until it is over. What looked like a new beginning is suddenly ended, and with no provision for further working through. You are encouraged to break free, but in all likelihood your encouragers won't be around to help when you try it. It is not surprising, then, that many participants cannot bear the sessions to end.

That is the way it is here in the "community." During the final half hour of the final session, the atmosphere borders on hysteria. It is the hour of desperation, the last chance to grab for an intense experience before the dispersal. It is like a singles bar at the end of a Friday night. People are trying to make a connection, trying to make something happen. Some, like Carmel, are rushing from group to group seeking attention; some are in a state of panic. They simply cannot believe that the community is coming to an end! It is too soon! They aren't ready! Their needs haven't been met! Some are trying to get in a last word with Dr. Rogers, to thank him for his presence, to let him know he has touched them.

Others seem simply dazed by this close encounter of the Third Force kind. They don't seem to know what to do. Still others, old pros perhaps, are calmly smiling, hugging, making for the door. They have the knowledge born of long years as quiet revolutionaries. Life is ebb and flow. They have no doubt that the process will go on.